Mr. President
A Book of U.S. Presidents

George Sullivan

D0064070

SCHOLASTIC INC.
New York Toronto London Auckland Sydney

Photo Credits:
Cover: George Bush at the President's desk in the Oval Office by
    AP/Wide World
Presidential Portraits: General Mills, Inc. (Official White House
    Photo: 157)
AP/Wide World: 6, 9, 12, 18, 19, 22, 36, 127, 135
The Bettmann Archive: 108
Ernest Ray Denmark, Esq.: 66
Denver Public Library, Western History Dept.: 92
The Thomas Alva Edison Foundation: 82
Essex Institute: 62
Ford Motor Company: 105
Alex Gardner: 71
Library of Congress: 59
Museum of the American Indian, Heye Foundation: 48
Museum of the City of New York: 20, 89
NASA: 144
National Archives: 78, 124
National Gallery of Art, Lloyd Ostendorf Collection: 69
The National Park Service, U.S. Dept. of Interior: 100
New York Public Library, Picture Collection: 65, 87
New York Public Library, Schomberg Collection: 39
The New York Times: 115
Smithsonian Institution: 95
UPI: 8, 11, 14, 123, 132, 140, 150, 154
UPI/Bettmann Archive: 3

ISBN 0-590-46540-6

Copyright © 1992, 1989, 1984 by George Sullivan.
All rights reserved. Published by Scholastic Inc.

12 11 10 9 8 7 6 5 4 3 2 1   2 3 4 5 6 7/9

Printed in the U.S.A.   28

Contents

John F. Kennedy taking Oath of Office as President of United States from Chief Justice Earl Warren; new Vice-President Lyndon B. Johnson, right.

Some Facts About
ELECTING THE PRESIDENT

Every four years, on January 20, a new or a reelected President of the United States is sworn into office. With his left hand on an open Bible and his right hand raised, he takes the Oath of Office from the Chief Justice of the United States.

This inauguration ceremony is the result of plans and actions that had their beginnings many months before — sometimes years before. A number of people may declare themselves candidates for the presidency. Whatever their qualifications, however, candidates must first win the nomination of their political party. They will debate, speak before various groups, and meet the public and the press on various issues. Once nominated, a candidate must campaign for election, seeking to win the approval of the voters. From nomination to inauguration is, today, a long, hard fight.

Who Can Become President

The Constitution says that a candidate for the presidency must be a United States citizen from birth. (A naturalized citizen cannot be a candidate.) A candidate must also be at least 35 years old and have lived in the United States for at least 14 years. (These are the *requirements*. To qualify, most presidential candidates will have proved their leadership, usually through their record in public office.)

How a Candidate Is Nominated

To be chosen as a candidate, a person must run against one or more other members of his or her party. The two major political parties, the Democrats and Republicans, use primary elections and national conventions in selecting their nominees.

The Primaries

From the late winter through the spring each election year, some thirty states hold presidential primaries. In a presidential primary, a party conducts an election among its members to choose delegates to the national convention. Each candidate who enters the primary offers a slate of delegates who have promised to support the candidate. When party members vote for the delegates, they are, in effect, voting for the candidate.

New Hampshire is the first state to hold a presidential primary. Candidates trudge through the snow and freezing temperatures to meet and talk with the New Hampshire voters, presenting their views and goals.

Former Vice-President Walter Mondale, campaigning in Concord, NH in early February, 1984, stands beside an ice sculpture of himself.

The Conventions

Late in the summer, Democratic and Republican delegates assemble for their national conventions, held at different times in separate cities. A convention is a political circus, complete with wild cheering, parading delegates, and stirring speech making.

The delegates first adopt a "platform," a statement of the party's principles and goals. The platform is made to appeal to many people and attract their votes.

After adopting the platform, delegates turn to nominating their candidate. Several names are usually put into nomination and then the voting begins. Ballots are taken until one person has more than one half of the delegates' votes. That person is the party's choice for President.

In early March, 1984, Senator Gary Hart campaigns in Boston, MA.

The same nominating and voting procedure is used in selecting a Vice-President. However, each party allows the newly nominated presidential candidate to name his or her own running mate.

Small-Party Candidates

Usually one or more of the smaller parties run candidates for President, too. In 1980, for example, the Independent Party was one of the smaller parties to offer a candidate. John Anderson, the Independent Party candidate, received about five and a half million votes, or six and a half percent of the total number of votes cast.

While no small-party candidate has ever won an election, these parties play an important role. They give voters a chance to express ideas or opinions that have not been put forth by candidates representing the major parties.

The Campaign

Once a candidate has won his party's nomination, he begins mapping campaign strategy. He states his position on various current issues. He steps up efforts to raise money and recruit volunteer workers.

Traveling by jet plane, the candidate

crisscrosses the country, making speeches to explain what he plans to do if elected. A big staff of policy advisers, media specialists, speech writers, and secretaries goes along. Everywhere the candidate and his or her staff go, they are accompanied by reporters and photographers.

The Campaign and Television

Television plays an important role in the campaign. Candidates try to provide a daily "news event" that will be telecast in the evening news programs. They also spend millions of dollars for television commercials.

The candidates also debate on television. John F. Kennedy and Richard M. Nixon were the first candidates to take part in televised debates. That was in 1960. All candidates since have followed the practice.

One of the 1960 Nixon-Kennedy television debates.

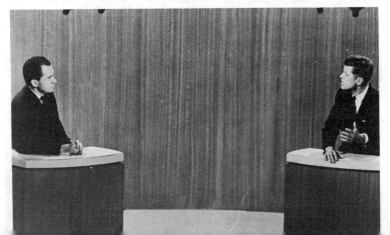

Election Day

Election Day is the first Tuesday after the first Monday in November. It is a legal holiday in most states.

Voters all over the nation go to the "polls," which are rooms in designated buildings in neighborhood districts called voting "precincts." In many towns, a voter receives a ballot from an election clerk. He or she takes the ballot into a private booth and marks the ballot, folds it, and then slips it into a ballot box.

Over half of the nation's voters cast ballots by voting machines. Standing in a curtained booth, the voter turns pointers or levers to indicate the candidate of his or her choice.

Lining up to vote in Smyrna, Georgia in 1966.

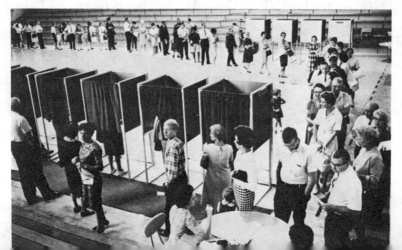

When the polling places close at the end of the day, the votes are counted. Paper ballots must be counted by hand. Machine votes can be tabulated automatically. The result makes up what is called the "popular vote."

The Electoral Vote*

Some people do not realize it, but when they cast their ballots they are not voting directly for the President. They are actually voting for presidential "electors" from their state.

Each state has a certain number of electors. The number is the same as the total of the state's Senators and Representatives in Congress. California, New York, and Texas have more electoral votes than any of the other states; California has 54, New York 33, and Texas 32. Alaska, Delaware, North Dakota, Montana, South Dakota, Vermont, and Wyoming each have three votes, as does the District of Columbia.

On Election Day, the candidate who gets the highest number of popular votes in a state gets *all* of that state's electoral votes. For example, in 1988 this was the popular vote in California.

Candidate	Number of Votes
George Bush	5,054,917
Michael Dukakis	4,702,233

*See page 160 for each state's number of electors.

Ronald Reagan greeting young admirers in 1980; Nancy Reagan, right.

Since Bush got the most votes, he received all 47 of California's electoral votes. (California had 47 electors in 1988.)

There are a total of 538 electoral votes (equal to the total number of Senators and Representatives the states send to Congress). The candidate who receives a majority of the electoral votes is the winner. If no candidate gets a majority, the House of Representatives chooses the President from the three candidates who have the highest number of electoral votes.

Inauguration Day

At noon on the January 20th following Election Day, the new President stands on the Capitol steps in Washington, D. C., and takes the Oath of Office. At the moment he takes the oath, he becomes the President of the United States.

Oath of Office

"**I** do solemnly swear (or affirm) that I will faithfully execute the Office of President of the United States, and will, to the best of my ability, preserve, protect, and defend the Constitution of the United States."

— from Article II, Section 1, U.S. Constitution

What the President Does

The Constitution grants the President enormous powers. Those powers have grown through the years. Today, the President of the United States is the most powerful elected official in the world.

As the nation's Chief Executive, it is the President's job to make sure all federal laws are enforced. He makes proposals for new laws and urges Congress to act upon them.

The President is Commander in Chief of the Army, Navy, Air Force, and Marines. He speaks for our country in dealing with foreign nations.

The President nominates Supreme Court judges, ambassadors, and other high officials. These nominations must be approved by the majority rule of the Senate.

Veto Power of the President

For the same reason, the power to make laws is shared by the President and Congress. When Congress passes a law, the President can either sign it or veto it. His veto kills the law unless Congress re-passes it by a two-thirds vote. Vetoes are seldom overridden.

As leader of his political party, the President has taken on powers not spelled out in the Constitution. For example, most Presidents have enough control within their party to get themselves renominated easily.

If a President does not choose to run, he can usually pick a candidate to run in his place.

The President and Television

The power of the presidency has also increased because of television. It gives the President the opportunity of reaching tens of millions of people directly in their homes, to ask for their support.

When the President greets foreign heads of state in the White House, presents awards or decorations, or talks to the winning coach on the telephone after the Super Bowl, television is there. Newspapers and magazines keep their attention focused on the White House, too. The President is always in the public eye, a big advantage in an election year.

The President's Staff

No one person could possibly handle all the President's duties without help. The Executive Office staff shoulders much of the burden.

This staff includes the President's Chief of Staff and other advisers; his press secretary, speech writers, and social secretaries; his physician and military aides; and the White House maintenance staff.

There are also several Executive Agencies that include the National Security Council, the Central Intelligence Agency (C.I.A.), and others.

The Cabinet

Also to assist the President are the heads of 14 executive departments of the government. When these 14 officials meet as a group, they are known as the Cabinet. The Cabinet offices are:

Secretary of State

Secretary of the Treasury

Secretary of Defense

Attorney General

Secretary of the Interior

Secretary of Agriculture

Secretary of Commerce

Secretary of Labor

Secretary of Health and Human Services

Secretary of Housing and Urban Development

Secretary of Transportation

Secretary of Energy

Secretary of Education

Secretary of Veterans Affairs

President Reagan meeting with cabinet members in January, 1981.

Jimmy Carter, as President elect, waving from Air Force jet at Albany, Georgia airport on November 6, 1976.

Presidential Travel

When the President travels, key staff members go with him. He keeps in touch with the White House by private telephone. On long vacations, the President may set up a "temporary White House," as President Truman did at Key West, Florida.

But no matter where he goes, the official problems go along, too. The person in the White House never escapes being President.

Our first President's first Inauguration took place at Federal Hall in New York City, which was then the nation's capital.

George Washington

1st President

Born: February 22, 1732

Birthplace: Pope's Creek, Westmoreland County, Virginia

Previous experience: Surveyor, farmer, delegate to Continental Congress, first Commander in Chief

Political party: Federalist

Term of office: April 30, 1789 – March 3, 1797

Died: December 14, 1799

Some people wanted George Washington to be King George of the new United States. But Washington had just fought a long war to free America from a king's tight rule. He wanted no kings in America, and he wanted to set a good precedent as the nation's first leader. Very soon, the proper title for the nation's chief executive became "Mr. President."

Born on the family farm in Virginia, young Washington was raised on land which his great-grandfather, a native of England, had settled. At 15, he was a big-boned young man who was good in arithmetic; he became a surveyor. Later, he commanded the colony's soldiers guarding Virginia's frontiers against French and Indian raiders. When the raids developed into the French and Indian War, Washington became an aide to British General Braddock. At 27, he had married Martha Curtis, a young widow with two children, and he looked forward to life as a gentleman farmer. Like many colonists, however, Washington suffered from British regulations and taxes, and he spoke out firmly against them.

On Christmas day in 1776, with British troops quartered in Philadelphia, Washington led his army across the Delaware River to New Jersey and took 1,400 Hessian soldiers by surprise early on December 26th.

And when the growing American resistance was met by British troops, America's Second Continental Congress called for military force. The Congress elected Washington to be Commander in Chief of the American forces. For seven long years, Washington held together his ragtag army — now slipping away from the enemy to launch a surprise attack; now retreating, in the winter cold, to Valley Forge. Many soldiers gave up and went home. But Washington hung on, losing more battles than he won. Eventually, with French aid, he forced the British to surrender.

Washington turned with relief to his beloved home and long-neglected farm at Mount Vernon, Virginia. But he realized that if the new nation was to be strong, it needed a binding contract with all the states. Washington called for a Constitutional Convention to meet in Philadelphia in 1787, to write the Constitution.

After the Constitution was approved by the states, the graying hero, 57 years old, was unanimously elected the country's first President. Washington chose two famous men to help him. Thomas Jefferson became America's first Secretary of State and Alexander Hamilton the first Secretary of the Treasury.

At last, after serving two terms, a worn and weary Washington retired to Mount Vernon for good. As its first Commander in Chief, President, and founder, Washington had been a true father of our country, helping it grow from 13 separate colonies into a free nation.

George Washington Important Events

- Department of Foreign Affairs (State Department), Department of War, Treasury Department, Post Office Department, and Office of the Attorney General established (1789)
- First session of U.S. Supreme Court (1790)
- First U.S. census authorized (1790)
- District of Columbia established (1791)
- Vermont admitted as the 14th state (1791)
- First ten amendments to the Constitution — the Bill of Rights — ratified (1791)
- Kentucky admitted as the 15th state (1792)
- Cornerstone of the White House laid (1792)
- Cornerstone of the Capitol laid (1793)
- Eli Whitney patented the cotton gin (1794)
- Tennessee admitted as the 16th state (1796)

John Adams

2nd President

Born: October 30, 1735

Birthplace: Braintree, Massachusetts

Previous experience: Lawyer, delegate to
Continental Congress, diplomat, Vice-President

Political party: Federalist

Term of office: March 4, 1797 – March 3, 1801

Died: July 4, 1826

A short, plump New Englander, John Adams was responsible for many noteworthy achievements during America's struggle for freedom. But because he lived in an age of great leaders, he was frequently overshadowed in what he did.

Harvard-educated lawyer John Adams was a patriot in Massachusetts in the years before the Revolution, although his fiery cousin, Samuel Adams, made a bigger stir. Typical of John Adams's sense of justice, he defended in court the British soldiers who fired into a patriotic Boston mob, because he felt everyone deserved a fair trial.

In the Continental Congress, he was assigned to the committee to write the Declaration of Independence. He had led the movement for such a declaration. But he was upstaged by Thomas Jefferson, who actually penned the great document.

As a diplomat in France during the Revolutionary War, Adams was outshone by the urbane and genial Benjamin Franklin. However, Adams helped negotiate the treaty of peace and was later a minister to the court of St. James in England.

Finally, Adams was the nation's first Vice-President — to the great President Washington. "The most insignificant office that ever the invention of man contrived," Adams wrote of his job to his beloved wife, Abigail.

Adams became President in 1797 — a very troubled time for the young nation. France attacked some of our ships. Many people, led by Alexander Hamilton, wanted Adams to declare war against France. But he resolutely held that the young nation should not fight. He sent a peace mission to France, a decision that may have cost him reelection.

Adams was the first President to live in the new capital city of Washington, D.C., and the first to occupy the White House. Only six rooms were ready when he and his wife moved in. Mrs. Adams hung her washing in the empty East Room.

When Adams's single term of office ended, he retired to his farm in Quincy, Massachusetts. He lived long enough to see a son, John Quincy, become President.

Adams wrote many letters to Jefferson. The friendly rivalry of these two patriots ended suddenly in 1826, when both men died on the Fourth of July.

John Adams
Important Events

- First naval vessel, *United States*, launched in Philadelphia (1797)
- Mississippi Territory created (1798)
- Navy Department created (1798)
- Marine Corps created (1798)
- Library of Congress established (1800)
- Capital moved to Washington, D.C. (1800)

Thomas Jefferson

3rd President

Born: April 13, 1743

Birthplace: Shadwell, Virginia

Previous experience: Delegate to Continental Congress, governor, diplomat, Secretary of State, Vice-President

Political party: Democratic-Republican

Term of office: March 4, 1801 – March 3, 1809

Died: July 4, 1826

For forty years, the remarkable Thomas Jefferson devoted himself to public service — and he also found time to be a successful lawyer, farmer, architect, musician, inventor.

Jefferson had many skills. He spoke six languages, including Latin and Greek. He loved gadgets and once built a clock that ran on cannon balls as weights. The tall, red-headed Jefferson could break a horse, dance a minuet, and play the violin.

He was admired as a writer and a thinker. In 1776 he was picked to head the Declaration of Independence committee, and Jefferson wrote the draft himself. Proclaiming "all men are created equal," the Declaration is often called the most important document in American history.

Three years later, Governor Jefferson established religious liberty in Virginia and introduced free education and public libraries in that state.

Thomas Jefferson drafting the Declaration of Independence in 1776.

When Jefferson became President, he sent Monroe and Livingstone to France to arrange the purchase of New Orleans and West Florida. Napoleon, who needed war funds, offered and sold the men an enormous tract of land that ran from the Mississippi River to the Rocky Mountains. This real estate bargain, at three cents per acre, was called the Louisiana Purchase; it doubled the size of the country. Jefferson also ordered the Lewis and Clark expedition to explore what is now the northwest part of the United States.

After leaving the presidency, Jefferson retired to Monticello, the home he had designed, and devoted his years to the founding of the University of Virginia.

One of the best tributes ever paid to Jefferson came from one of his presidential successors — John F. Kennedy. Kennedy was playing host to a group of men and women who had been honored for their outstanding achievements in art and science. Kennedy described his guests as the most extraordinary collection of talent that had ever been gathered together at the White House, with the possible exception of Thomas Jefferson — when he dined alone.

Thomas Jefferson
Important Events

- U.S. Military Academy authorized (1802)
- Ohio admitted as 17th state (1803)
- Louisiana Purchase treaty signed (1803)
- Lewis and Clark left St. Louis on their expedition to the Pacific (1803)
- Robert Fulton's steamboat, the *Clermont*, made trip on Hudson River in New York (1807)
- Illinois Territory established (1809)

Monticello, the beautiful home in Virginia which Jefferson designed and built, stands today as a monument to his varied interests and talents.

James Madison

4th President

Born: March 16, 1751
Birthplace: Port Conway, Virginia
Previous experience: Lawyer, delegate to Continental Congress, Congressman, Secretary of State
Political party: Democratic-Republican
Term of office: March 4, 1809 – March 3, 1817
Died: June 28, 1836

One of our smallest Presidents, the brilliant Virginian, James Madison, stood only 5-foot-4 and never weighed more than 100 pounds. At his inauguration, he looked like a little old man beside his blooming wife, Dolley. Yet Madison was one of the "Big Four" from Virginia. Like Monroe, Jefferson, and Washington, he helped lead Congress and the nation during America's formative years.

Right after the Revolutionary War, the states began quarreling among themselves. Madison believed we needed a strong national government to survive. More than anyone else, he created the Constitution and urged its adoption by the states.

Madison also fought to add the first ten amendments to the Constitution. Known as the "Bill of Rights," these amendments protect such liberties as freedom of speech, freedom of the press, freedom of religion, and the right to have a trial by jury.

This work was all behind Madison when, in 1794, at the age of 43, he met and married a young and pretty widow, Dolley Payne Todd. When Madison took over as President in 1809, Dolley became a popular hostess, known for her gala parties. At these parties, many people had their first taste of a new dessert called "ice cream."

During Madison's first term as President, the young nation's ships were seized at sea by warring France and England. America's quarrel with England over freedom of the seas led to the War of 1812. In a surprise raid on Washington, British marines set fire to public buildings and burned the Executive Mansion. Madison and his wife fled to the Virginia woods. Dolley paused long enough to carry away a valuable portrait of George Washington.

When the Madisons returned to Washington after the war, they had to live in temporary quarters until the Executive Mansion was rebuilt.

White paint was used to cover the fire-blackened exterior, and from then on it was known as the "White House."

Retiring from the White House in 1817, Madison returned to his home in Montpelier, Virginia. He died in 1836 at the age of 85; he had outlived all the other founders of the nation.

James Madison
Important Events

- General William Henry Harrison defeated Indian attackers at battle of Tippecanoe (1811)
- Louisiana admitted as the 18th state (1812)
- Missouri Territory organized (1812)
- War declared against Great Britain (1812)
- "The Star-Spangled Banner" composed by Francis Scott Key (1814)
- Peace treaty signed with Great Britain (1814)
- Indiana admitted as 19th state (1816)

James Monroe

5th President

Born: April 28, 1758

Birthplace: Westmoreland County, Virginia

Previous experience: Soldier, lawyer, delegate to Continental Congress, Senator, governor, diplomat, Secretary of State, Secretary of War

Political party: Democratic-Republican

Term of office: March 4, 1817 – March 3, 1825

Died: July 4, 1831

James Monroe always seemed to be where the action was.

When the Revolutionary War broke out, Monroe was 18. A Virginia planter's son, he was attending William and Mary College, but quit school to join General Washington's army in New York. Six months later, as Lieutenant Monroe, he crossed the Delaware with Washington and then fought in the hard battles of Brandywine, Germantown, and Monmouth. At Trenton, a bullet struck him and remained in his shoulder for the rest of his life.

After the Revolution, Monroe studied law with Thomas Jefferson and entered politics. He was elected U.S. Senator, then became Minister to France and helped negotiate the Louisiana Purchase, by which France sold America enough land to double the size of our country. Back home, Monroe was twice elected governor of Virginia, and later served as Secretary of State.

The popular Monroe was elected President in 1816, and reelected in 1820 almost unanimously by an electoral vote of 231 to 1. (The

The "Savannah" was the first American ship to make the transatlantic crossing under steam power. Starting from Savannah, GA on May 22, 1819, the trip to Liverpool, England took 29 days. (Early steamships carried sails.)

single vote against him was cast by a New Hampshire delegate who wanted George Washington to have the honor of being the only unanimous choice in history.)

As President, Monroe's greatest successes took place in the field he knew best — foreign policy. When Spain cast a longing eye on Central and South American countries that had become newly independent, Monroe told the Spanish and other European nations, "Hands off." He declared that the United States would permit no "foreign interference" in the New World. We remember James Monroe best for this "Monroe Doctrine."

James Monroe
Important Events

- Mississippi admitted as the 20th state (1817)
- Illinois admitted as the 21st state (1818)
- Florida purchased from Spain (1819)
- First American steamship crossed the Atlantic (1819)
- Alabama admitted as the 22nd state (1819)
- Maine admitted as 23rd state (1820)
- Missouri admitted as 24th state (1821)
- Monroe Doctrine proclaimed (1823)

John Quincy Adams

6th President

Born: July 11, 1767

Birthplace: Braintree, Massachusetts

Previous experience: Lawyer, diplomat, Senator, Secretary of State, Congressman

Political party: Democratic-Republican

Term of office: March 4, 1825 – March 3, 1829

Died: February 23, 1848

John Quincy Adams was the only President who was also the son of a President. His father was John Adams.

Both Adamses were born in Braintree, Massachusetts, in houses that stood next to each other. They both went to Harvard College, became lawyers, and lived in the same house in their later years. Both were short and as stubborn as mules.

Both served as diplomats, helping to write peace treaties to end wars with England — John Adams after the Revolutionary War, and John Quincy Adams after the War of 1812, and each served only one term as President.

John Quincy Adams was one of the great Secretaries of State. Serving under Monroe, he made agreements on lands with Spain and England, and helped Monroe formulate the Monroe Doctrine.

As President, John Quincy Adams lived a plain life. He rose each morning at five o'clock, built his own fire, read his Bible, and bathed in the Potomac — before anyone else in the capital was awake. One time, while he was taking his morning dip, a thief ran off with his clothes. The President had to ask a passing boy to dash up to the White House and ask Mrs. Adams for something to wear.

Slaves carrying cotton they have picked in the fields. With the growth of cloth mills in the North and in England, and invention of the cotton gin, cotton became the Southern crop.

Adams had a troubled term in office. He had to work with a hostile Congress that blocked most of his plans. His program to encourage interest and education in the arts and sciences had some success, however. He was able to get the important Smithsonian Institution established.

Adams was defeated for reelection by Andrew Jackson in 1828. But he was not retired for long. When his neighbors asked him if he would be willing to represent their district in Congress, Adams said yes.

The debate on slavery was beginning to heat up. With Adams in Congress, it got much hotter. He hated slavery. For eight years, he argued in Congress against owning slaves. Other Congressmen, not wanting to hear about the touchy subject, tried to silence him.

Adams kept talking — until one day in 1848. At the age of 80, while waiting for still another chance to speak in the House of Representatives on slavery, Adams collapsed from a stroke. Two days later he died.

John Quincy Adams Important Events

- Erie Canal opened for traffic (1825)
- Construction began on Baltimore & Ohio railroad (1828)

Andrew Jackson

7th President

Born: March 15, 1767

Birthplace: Waxhaw District, South Carolina

Previous experience: Lawyer, Congressman, military
leader, governor, Senator

Political party: Democratic

Term of office: March 4, 1829 – March 3, 1837

Died: June 8, 1845

After General Andrew Jackson won the presidency in 1828, the farmers, working men, and frontiersmen who supported him swarmed to Washington. They perched on rooftops and packed sidewalks to catch a glimpse of him on Inauguration Day. After the ceremony, these men in their coonskin caps and muddy boots pushed their way into the White House. They toppled punch bowls and stood on satin-covered chairs to cheer the new President. "The reign of King Mob," one observer called it.

No doubt about it, Andrew Jackson gave a new direction to the presidency. From Washington to John Quincy Adams, the Presidents had been gentlemen of money and privilege. Jackson changed that. He represented the plain, common people.

Jackson was the first President to be born in a log cabin and the first from the new West. As an unschooled orphan of 13, he fought in the Revolutionary War. When he was taken prisoner, he refused to clean a British officer's boots, and for that he received a saber blow that left a scar on his forehead for life.

At the age of 20, Jackson was a backwoods lawyer. Ten years later, he was a strong political figure in the newly formed state of Tennessee, and held the office of U.S. Senator.

In the War of 1812, the hot-headed, hawk-nosed Jackson became a national hero, first as an Indian fighter, and then in the Battle of New Orleans.

After his great victory over the British at New Orleans, people began mentioning Jackson as a future President. In 1824 he was defeated by John Quincy Adams, but four years later Jackson beat Adams by a clear margin. At his moment of glory, however, Jackson was plunged into sorrow. His beloved wife, Rachel, died just as Jackson was preparing to leave for Washington.

In his first year as President, Jackson removed some two thousand federal office-holders and gave their jobs to his followers. He battled the Bank of the United States, calling it a bank of the rich.

Jackson was a Southerner, but when the Southern state of South Carolina threatened to leave the Union in a squabble over tariffs, Jackson would not permit it. "Our Union — it must be preserved," he declared.

Reelected in 1832, Jackson continued his fight as the people's champion. Four years later he retired to the home he had built near Nashville, Tennessee — the Hermitage. There he lies in a simple grave.

Andrew Jackson
Important Events

- Arkansas admitted as the 25th state (1836)
- Wisconsin Territory organized (1836)
- Republic of Texas recognized (1836)
- Michigan admitted as the 26th state (1837)

Martin Van Buren

8th President

Born: December 5, 1782

Birthplace: Kinderhook, New York

Previous experience: Lawyer, Senator, governor, Secretary of State, Vice-President

Political party: Democratic

Term of office: March 4, 1837 – March 3, 1841

Died: July 24, 1862

Our first seven Presidents were born in what had been Colonial America. Martin Van Buren was the first President born in the new United States. Even so, "Little Van" grew up speaking Dutch better than English. His ancestors came from the Netherlands, and he was raised in the old Dutch village of Kinderhook, New York.

His father owned a tavern that was a convenient stopping place for politicians traveling from New York City to Albany, and young Van Buren met the political leaders of the day there. At 14, he took a job as a law clerk, and at 20, he set up his own successful law practice.

Van Buren was even more successful as a politician. He was always ready with a smile, a handshake, and a joke. He became so skilled in achieving his political goals that he was nicknamed the "Little Magician."

In 1828 Van Buren worked his magic for Andrew Jackson, helping him to become President. In turn, Jackson made Van Buren his Secretary of State and later, his Vice-President. Jackson also supported him when Van Buren ran for the Presidency in 1836.

Van Buren had been in office only two months when the nation was struck by the financial panic of 1837. Banks closed one after another, mill towns shut down and workers lost their jobs. The unemployed rioted in New York. Van Buren, believing the government should not interfere in private business, did little to help.

By the time Van Buren sought reelection in 1840, he was terribly unpopular. To make matters worse, his rivals portrayed him as a man who drank wine from a silver goblet and ate his meals from gold plates. His opponent, William Henry Harrison, won easily.

Van Buren, the politician, never regained the support of the Democratic Party. He was nominated by the Free Soil Party — a party opposed to slavery — in 1848. He did not win, however, and did not try again.

Martin Van Buren
Important Events

- Patent for manufacture of rubber obtained by Charles Goodyear (1837)
- Boundary treaty with Texas signed (1838)
- Iowa territorial government authorized (1838)

William Henry Harrison

9th President

Born: February 9, 1773

Birthplace: Berkeley, Virginia

Previous experience: Military leader, territorial governor, Congressman, Senator

Political party: Whig*

Term of office: March 4, 1841 – April 4, 1841

Died: April 4, 1841

Like Andrew Jackson, William Henry Harrison won fame because of his success as an Indian fighter and as a general during the War of 1812.

Born in Virginia, Harrison was the youngest child in a family of seven children. At 14, he entered college to study medicine, but had to give up his medical studies when his father died. He joined the Army and headed to the northwest Indian frontier.

In 1801 Harrison became governor of the Indiana Territory (now Indiana and Illinois), and he held that post for 12 years. His main task was

*Party established about 1834 to oppose the Democrats.

47

to obtain title to Indian lands for settlers moving west into the wilderness, and to defend the settlements against Indian raids.

The frontier Indians were up in arms because many millions of acres of hunting ground had been closed to them. Harrison met with their leaders and tried to cool their anger but without success. Under the great Shawnee chief, Tecum-

Tecumseh, a Shawnee chief, became a great leader of the Indians, whose treaties with the settlers were being constantly broken. With his brother "the Prophet," Tecumseh organized a confederation of Indian tribes that fought the settlers' takeover of Indian land.

seh, the Indians formed a close confederation, and the raids continued against the settlers.

In 1811, with a force of about 800 volunteers, Harrison was headed toward an Indian town when the Indians attacked his camp on Tippecanoe Creek. Harrison repulsed them and later crushed Tecumseh's confederation. After the victory at Tippecanoe, "Old Tippecanoe" Harrison was hailed as a national hero.

Harrison served as a Congressman and Senator, and in 1840 the Whigs settled on Harrison as a presidential candidate. Their campaign slogan was "Tippecanoe and Tyler, too." (John Tyler was the vice-presidential candidate.) Harrison and Tyler won in a landslide.

The day of Harrison's inauguration was cold and rainy. Harrison, at 68, wanted to show he was in good health. He rode on horseback in the parade for two hours and took the Oath of Office bareheaded.

As a result, Harrison caught a cold that developed into pneumonia. He died on April 4, 1841, only 32 days after his inauguration. Harrison was the first President to die in office.

Nothing of note happened in the United States during the 32 days Harrison was in office.

John Tyler

10th President

Born: March 29, 1790

Birthplace: Charles City County, Virginia

Previous experience: Lawyer, Congressman, governor, Senator, Vice-President

Political party: Whig

Term of office: April 6, 1841 – March 3, 1845

Died: January 18, 1862

John Tyler was the son of a plantation owner. A mild-mannered boy, he wrote and read poetry and enjoyed playing the violin. But he grew into a strong-minded, strong-willed adult. As President, he often opposed the leaders of Congress and his party.

Tyler was only 17 when he graduated from the College of William and Mary, and by 19, he was a practicing lawyer. Then he entered politics. After serving as a Congressman, governor, and Senator, Tyler became Vice-President in the election of 1840.

When President William Henry Harrison died a month after being inaugurated, Tyler became the first Vice-President to become President. At the time, some said that Tyler was only "Acting President." But Tyler insisted he be given the full title and granted full powers of office. Ever since then, on the death of the President, the Vice-President has been sworn in with full executive powers.

As President, Tyler's firmness soon brought him into conflict with Henry Clay and other leaders of his party. The Whigs wanted to set up a new national bank. They wanted high taxes on

The "Sea Witch," one of the streamlined clipper ships designed for the China tea trade, set an all-time record for sailing ships: 74 days between Canton, China and New York in 1848–1849. Thirty years after steamboats first spanned the Atlantic, the clipper ships made record sailings to China, to Australia's gold fields, and to San Francisco (around Cape Horn).

imported goods. When Tyler opposed these ideas, his Cabinet resigned and the Whigs ousted Tyler. He was a President without a party.

Strong-minded President Tyler brought the war with the Seminole Indians in Florida to an end. He also entered into a treaty with China, which opened the way for trade with the countries of the Far East.

Tyler was the first President whose wife died while he was in office. When he remarried, he became the first President to marry while in office. He had fifteen children; no President has had more.

In 1845 Tyler retired to his estate in Virginia. When he died, he was still considered a rebel by the Whig leaders, who refused to make an official announcement of his death.

John Tyler
Important Events

- Treaty signed with Great Britain, settling U.S.-Canadian border in Maine and Minnesota Territory (1842)
- First message sent over first telegraph line (1844)
- Florida admitted as the 27th state (March 3, 1845)

James Knox Polk

11th President

Born: November 2, 1795
Birthplace: Mecklenburg County, North Carolina
Previous experience: Lawyer, Congressman, governor
Political party: Democratic
Term of office: March 4, 1845 – March 3, 1849
Died: June 15, 1849

"**O**ne of the very best, most honest, and most successful Presidents the country ever had," was the way one historian described James Polk.

Polk was born in North Carolina and raised on the Tennessee frontier. In college, he never missed a class, and in his fourteen years as Congressman, he was absent only once. He became Speaker of the House and was considered by most to be fair yet firm.

In 1844 Polk ran for President against the famous Senator Henry Clay. Polk was so little known that he was called a "dark horse." (At the race track, a "dark horse" is an unknown that unexpectedly wins.) In the election Polk squeezed out a victory over Clay.

When Polk took office, there were only 27 states in the Union. Much of the country was still Indian territory or claimed by foreign countries. "All of Texas and all of Oregon" had been Polk's campaign slogan. He settled the Oregon border by a treaty with Great Britain. But the dispute with Mexico over the Texas border was not settled so easily.

Two prospectors pan for gold. Gold was discovered in California in January, 1848. By 1849, 80,000 prospectors were pouring into the "Golden State."

Polk sent troops into the disputed area. When they were fired upon, Polk was able to announce, "War exists by act of Mexico." American troops advanced into Mexican territory.

The Mexican War ended in 1848. Under the terms of the peace treaty, Mexico gave up all claims to Texas and territory that is now California and Nevada, and much of what is Arizona, Colorado, New Mexico, and Wyoming.

Polk made other efforts to expand the United States. He offered Spain $100 million for Cuba. But Spain turned down the offer.

Polk chose not to run for a second term and died only three months after he left office.

James Knox Polk
Important Events

- Texas admitted as 28th state (Dec. 29, 1845)
- U.S. declared war on Mexico (1846)
- Treaty concluded with Great Britain establishing Oregon boundary (1846)
- Iowa admitted as 29th state (1846)
- Gold discovered in California (1848)
- Wisconsin admitted as 30th state (1848)

Zachary Taylor

12th President

Born: November 24, 1784
Birthplace: Montebello, Orange County, Virginia
Previous experience: Military leader
Political party: Whig
Term of office: March 4, 1849 – July 9, 1850
Died: July 9, 1850

Zachary Taylor was the first military leader to become President without first holding other government posts. His father had been a colonel in the Revolution, and talk of battles flowed through the Taylor home.

At the age of 18, Taylor had a commission in the Army; he remained a soldier for the next forty years. He fought in the War of 1812 and in the Mexican War of 1846, and he fought against the Seminole Indians in Florida.

The Mexican War made Taylor a national hero. As the leader of 5,000 American volunteers, he defeated Santa Anna and a force nearly four times larger than his own.

Taylor did not look like a military hero. He was a squat little man who had to be boosted into his saddle. "Old Rough and Ready" preferred wearing the simple clothes of a farmer rather than a military uniform.

Taylor had little interest in politics. But the Whigs nominated him anyway—and he won. At the White House, he strolled about, shaking hands with anyone who stopped by. He let his old war horse graze on the White House lawn.

Although he was a slave owner, Taylor didn't want to see slavery extended into the territories won in the Mexican War. He also wanted New Mexico and California added to the Union as free — not slave — states.

Zachary Taylor was not President for very long. On the Fourth of July, 1850, 16 months after taking office, he took part in ceremonies at the then-unfinished Washington monument. The day was broiling hot. Taylor suffered a sunstroke and died, five days later.

Zachary Taylor
Important Event

- Clay Compromise passed, providing for the admission of California as a free state and the formation of the territories of New Mexico and Utah (1850)

Millard Fillmore

13th President

Born: January 7, 1800
Birthplace: Summerhill, New York
Previous experience: Lawyer, Congressman, Vice-President
Political party: Whig
Term of office: July 10, 1850 – March 3, 1853
Died: March 8, 1874

The day after President Zachary Taylor's death, his Vice-President, tall, handsome Millard Fillmore, took the Oath of Office.

Millard Fillmore was the son of a poor New York farmer. As a small boy, he helped his father clear land and raise crops. Then he was sent away to learn the clothmaker's trade. His master treated him so harshly that Millard borrowed $30 to purchase his freedom, then hiked over one hundred miles back to his log-cabin home.

Millard was 18 when he attended his first school. He fell in love with his school teacher, Abigail Powers. Seven years later, she became his wife.

At 23, Fillmore got a job as a law clerk and went on to become a lawyer. He was elected to the

New York State Assembly; and then became a U.S. Congressman. At the Whig Convention in 1848, when he was 48, Fillmore was chosen as the party's vice-presidential candidate.

During his term as President, Fillmore modernized the White House. A cast-iron stove replaced the huge fireplace that had been used for cooking. Plumbers put in the first White House bathtub with running water. When Abigail Fillmore set aside a White House room for a library, Congress granted her $250 to buy books.

President Fillmore saw the slavery issue grow dangerously hot. In the North, many people

The White House in President Fillmore's day.

wanted to end slavery, while many Southerners wanted to see slavery spread to the new Western states. Fillmore himself didn't have strong opinions on slavery. Then Congress passed the Fugitive Slave Act, making federal officials responsible for returning runaway slaves to their Southern masters. Fillmore could kill the bill by refusing to sign it, or put his signature to it, making it law. Fillmore signed.

This turned out to be a big mistake. Anti-slavery Northerners hated the new law. Mobs attacked federal marshals to free slaves they had captured.

The North never forgave Fillmore or the Whig Party, which died away.

Millard Fillmore
Important Events

- **California admitted as 31st state (1850)**
- **Fugitive Slave Act became law (1850)**
- **Washington Territory created out of northern half of Oregon (1853)**

Franklin Pierce

14th President

Born: November 23, 1804
Birthplace: Hillsborough, New Hampshire
Previous experience: Lawyer, Congressman, Senator
Political party: Democratic
Term of office: March 4, 1853 – March 3, 1857
Died: October 8, 1869

Franklin Pierce was among our youngest Presidents; he was only 48 when he was elected. Like President Fillmore, Pierce was a Northerner who was "soft" toward the South on slave issues. These men were called "dough-faces" because their opinions could be kneaded like dough by pro-slavery Southerners.

Young Franklin was educated in private schools and entered college at 15. In Bowdoin College, Maine, his classmates included the famous writers Nathaniel Hawthorne and Henry Wadsworth Longfellow.

After he graduated, Pierce studied law and went into politics, holding various state offices. He was elected to Congress, and in 1836, at the age of 32, he became the youngest Senator in Washington.

Pierce did not seek the presidency. His friends put his name in nomination when the Democratic convention became deadlocked. Although he made no campaign speeches, he won the election easily, defeating General Winfield Scott and the dying Whig party.

Pierce was handsome and fun-loving. But his life was scarred by tragedy. Two of his sons died in infancy. A third son, Benjamin, was 11

A portrait of young Nathaniel Hawthorne, who wrote *The Scarlet Letter* and *The House of Seven Gables* stories.

years old at the time Pierce was elected President. Just before his inauguration, Pierce, his wife, and his son were traveling by train from Boston to Concord, New Hampshire, when their railroad car was derailed and overturned. Pierce and his wife were only slightly injured, but young Benjamin was crushed to death.

Pierce's term as President was tinged with tragedy, too. He helped to get the Kansas-Nebraska Act passed. It allowed new settlers there to vote whether or not to have slavery, and that led to bloody fighting between the pro-slavery and anti-slavery groups—a foretaste of the Civil War.

At the Democratic National Convention in 1856, Pierce was rejected by his party in favor of James Buchanan, who was more neutral on the slavery question. Pierce returned to his New Hampshire home in bitterness.

Franklin Pierce Important Events

- Kansas-Nebraska Act passed, permitting state residents to decide slavery issue (1854)
- U.S. acquired border territories from Mexico through Gadsden Purchase (1854)

James Buchanan

15th President

Born: April 23, 1791

Birthplace: Cove Gap, Pennsylvania

Previous experience: Lawyer, Congressman, Senator, diplomat, Cabinet member

Political party: Democratic

Term of office: March 4, 1857 – March 3, 1861

Died: June 1, 1868

By the time James Buchanan became President, at 65, the nation was facing war over slavery. "Old Buck" had had 43 years of shining government experience, but it didn't help him in grappling with the grave problems of the day. He was old and tired and too cautious by nature to make hard decisions.

Buchanan was the oldest of eleven children. Born in a Pennsylvania log cabin, he learned arithmetic by helping out in his father's store. At 18 he graduated from Dickinson College, and before he was 30, he had made $300,000.

Buchanan studied law and built a very successful law practice. He was not so successful in love. Shortly after his bride-to-be broke their engagement over a misunderstanding, she died, and the heart-broken Buchanan never married. He turned, instead, to public service. He was a Congressman for ten years and a Senator for twelve years. Under Presidents Jackson, Polk, and Pierce, Buchanan was a top-level foreign diplomat.

By serving in foreign countries, Buchanan had avoided the bitter arguments about slavery, and this helped him to win the nomination at the Democratic National Convention in 1856.

Shortly after Buchanan became President, the Supreme Court handed down the fateful Dred Scott decision. Basically, it said that Con-

The Dred Scott decision meant that slave hunters could search for runaway slaves and take them from free states.

gress had no power to interfere with slavery. Northerners were furious and fought against the ruling.

But Buchanan refused to take sides. "You are sleeping on a volcano," he was warned. The slave-owning Southern states threatened to secede—that is, to leave the U.S.A. and form their own country—unless slavery was protected. Buchanan said that a state had no right to secede,

An old plantation home in Mississippi. Many slaves in Maryland and Virginia were "sold down the river" to cotton plantation owners in the deep South.

but that, on the other hand, the federal government had no legal right to stop a state from seceding.

In Buchanan's last months as President, South Carolina did secede, soon followed by six other states. They set up the "Confederate States of America" under Jefferson Davis. Still Buchanan did nothing.

Rejected by both sides, Buchanan left the White House in 1861. With great relief he handed over the reins of government to his successor, Abraham Lincoln, and slipped away to his Pennsylvania home.

James Buchanan
Important Events

- Dred Scott decision announced by Supreme Court (1857)
- Minnesota admitted as 32nd state (1858)
- Atlantic cable completed (1858)
- Oregon admitted as 33rd state (1859)
- Pony Express service began between St. Joseph, Missouri, and Sacramento, California (1860)
- South Carolina seceded from the Union (1860)
- Kansas admitted as 34th state (1861)
- Confederate States of America organized (1861)

Abraham Lincoln

16th President

Born: February 12, 1809
Birthplace: Hardin County, Kentucky
Previous experience: Lawyer, Congressman
Political party: Republican
Term of office: March 4, 1861 – April 15, 1865
Died: April 15, 1865

Abraham Lincoln led the fight to save the Union and end slavery. Although he had only a scant frontier education and little experience in public office, his keen judgment and deep sense of humanity made him one of our greatest Presidents.

Abraham Lincoln was born in a dirt-floor log cabin. The family was always poor. His father, a carpenter, never learned to read or write.

When Abe was almost eight, the Lincolns moved to Indiana. Less than two years later, his mother, Nancy Hanks, died of the "milk sickness," leaving Abe and his older sister, Sarah. His father remarried and Sarah Johnson became the new Mrs. Lincoln. A widow with three children of her own, she brought warmth to the family and encouraged young Abe to better himself. He called her his "best friend in this world."

At 16, Abe was tall, slim, and strong. He did odd jobs for anyone who would hire him. He worked as a farmhand, grocery clerk, and rail splitter, reading and studying whenever he could.

Lincoln reading to his youngest son, Tad.

He also worked as a deckhand on a flatboat that floated down the Ohio and Mississippi rivers to New Orleans. On one such trip he saw chained blacks being whipped and beaten. He hated slavery from that day.

Lincoln received his license to practice law in 1836, and began "traveling the circuit." He and other lawyers would ride on horseback from village to village, trying cases. The work sharpened his skills as a debater.

Lincoln was elected to Congress as a Whig in 1847. Then he quit politics and returned to Springfield, Illinois, to practice law again, becoming one of the best-known lawyers in Illinois. He was in his early 40s now, married to Mary Todd, and the father of four sons.

Lincoln turned his attention to politics a second time in 1855, speaking out against the Kansas-Nebraska Act that said people in the Western territories could have slavery if they voted for it.

Illinois Senator Stephen A. Douglas was the author of this act. In 1858 Lincoln left the Whigs to join the anti-slavery Republican Party. He wanted to run against Douglas for the Senate. Lincoln challenged Douglas to a series of debates. Although Lincoln lost the election, the debates made him nationally famous; he was nominated for the Presidency in 1860.

Within six weeks after Lincoln had taken office as President, Southern troops attacked Fort Sumter in the harbor of Charleston, South

Lincoln, at the battlefront, talks with Union Army officers.

Carolina. They shot down the flag and captured the fort. The next day Lincoln issued a call for 75,000 volunteers to retake the fort and other property now in Confederate hands. This was the start of the Civil War.

Lincoln was President throughout the war's four bitter years. In mid-1862 he issued his famous Emancipation Proclamation, which gave freedom to some three million blacks in the South.

Northern forces suffered one battlefield defeat after another in the early stages of the war. But in 1863 and 1864, the tide began to turn in the Union's favor. Lincoln was reelected in 1864.

When he took the Oath of Office, the war's end was in sight. Lincoln urged, instead of taking vengeance against the South, that there be "malice toward none" and "charity for all."

Tragically, Lincoln had no opportunity to put his postwar policies into effect. On April 14, 1865, five days after the surrender of Confederate forces, Lincoln was attending the theater with his wife, when a man named John Wilkes Booth crept up from behind and shot him in the head. The President died the next day. Speaking for the sorrowing nation, one Cabinet member said, "Now he belongs to the ages."

Abraham Lincoln
Important Events

- First attack in Civil War at Fort Sumter, South Carolina (1861)
- Battle between the *Monitor* and the *Merrimac* (1862)
- Emancipation Proclamation issued (1862)
- West Virginia admitted as 35th state (1863)
- Nevada admitted as 36th state (1864)
- General Robert E. Lee surrendered to General Ulysses S. Grant, ending Civil War (1865)

Andrew Johnson

17th President

Born: December 29, 1808

Birthplace: Raleigh, North Carolina

Previous experience: Tailor, Congressman, governor, Senator

Political party: Democratic

Term of office: April 15, 1865 – March 3, 1869

Died: July 31, 1875

With the death of President Lincoln, the presidency fell to Andrew Johnson, a southern Democrat whom Lincoln had picked to be his Vice-President in 1864. A convincing speaker, Andrew Johnson was largely self-taught. His parents had been too poor to send him to school. He learned to read and write while he was serving as apprentice to a tailor.

Later, Johnson set up as a tailor in Greeneville, Tennessee, and took part in debates at the local school. He married and became mayor of the town, then a Congressman. He was elected governor of Tennessee; and then at 49, he became a U.S. Senator.

Although a Southerner, Johnson was loyal to the Union cause and opposed secession. The other Southern Senators branded him a traitor. When the Civil War broke out, every Southern Senator quit and went back home—except Andrew Johnson.

In 1862 President Lincoln appointed Johnson military governor of Tennessee. And two years later, impressed by Johnson's moderate views, Lincoln chose him as his Vice-President.

Now President Johnson proceeded to "reconstruct" the ex-Confederate states while Congress was not in session. Many Northern members of Congress wanted to punish the Southerners as rebels and traitors. But Johnson pardoned all who would take an oath of allegiance. The struggle became more bitter as Congress passed bills over Johnson's veto.

Finally, when Johnson dismissed Secretary of War Stanton from his Cabinet without the permission of Congress, Congress acted to impeach him. Johnson went on trial, accused of "high crimes and misdemeanors."

The trial lasted two months. The House voted for impeachment, but the Senate was a single vote short of the two-thirds majority needed to remove a President from office. Johnson finished his term.

Johnson actually sought the presidential nomination again in 1868, but his party rejected him.

Finally, in 1874, he was elected to his old office as U.S. Senator from Tennessee. When he took his Senate seat, Johnson was loudly applauded in the very chamber where he had been tried only seven years before.

Andrew Johnson
Important Events

- **Thirteenth Amendment to the Constitution ratified, abolishing slavery (1865)**
- **Nebraska admitted as 37th state (1867)**
- **Secretary of State William H. Seward arranged to buy Alaska from Russia (1867)**
- **Fourteenth Amendment to the Constitution ratified, establishing rights of citizens (1868)**

Ulysses Simpson Grant

18th President

Born: April 27, 1822
Birthplace: Point Pleasant, Ohio
Previous experience: Military leader
Political party: Republican
Term of office: March 4, 1869 – March 3, 1877
Died: July 23, 1885

At the beginning of the Civil War, Hiram Ulysses Grant was an unknown clerk in a store. By the end of the war, as Ulysses Simpson Grant, he was the nation's most celebrated general.

The son of a farmer and tanner, young "Lyss" disliked both farming and tannery work. Horses were what he liked, and he rode like a champion.

Although his schooling had been irregular, it was enough to get Grant into the U.S. Military Academy at West Point, from which he graduated. In the Mexican War, Grant fought under General Zachary Taylor. He was cited for bravery and promoted to the rank of captain.

After the Mexican War, Grant found that his low Army pay was not enough to support his wife and family, so he resigned from the Army.

He tried farming, then sold real estate, and when that too failed, he went to work in his brother's leather shop.

A rare, informal photo of Grant, the soldier.

Then came the Civil War, and Grant rejoined the Army. In the East, the war was going badly for the Union forces, but in the West, Grant began winning victories, one after another.

This led President Lincoln to put him in command of all the Union armies, and Grant led the North to victory. It was spring when the Southern forces surrendered, and Grant let the Southern soldiers keep their horses so that they could do their spring plowing.

Grant was a national hero after the war. The Republicans picked him to run for President, and he won easily.

As President, Grant made errors of judgment that lost him the nation's respect. He appointed friends to high positions in the government; when they cheated, stole, and took bribes, the easy-going President got the blame.

After he left the presidency, Grant put his life savings into a banking firm. But his partner was a crook, and Grant lost all his money.

When Grant learned he was suffering from throat cancer, he courageously began to write his life story so that his wife would have money to live on. The book made the family rich. But Grant never knew that. Four days after he wrote the last word, he died.

Ulysses Simpson Grant
Important Events

- First transcontinental railroad service (1869)
- Alexander Graham Bell transmitted sound of human voice on the telephone (1876)
- General George Custer's forces destroyed by Indians led by Sitting Bull at Little Big Horn, Montana (1876)
- Colorado admitted to the Union as the 38th state (1876).

Rutherford Birchard Hayes

19th President

Born: October 4, 1822

Birthplace: Delaware, Ohio

Previous experience: Lawyer, military leader, Congressman, governor

Political party: Republican

Term of office: March 4, 1877 – March 3, 1881

Died: January 17, 1893

Although Rutherford B. Hayes nearly lost the election, he came to be respected by everyone as an honest, hard-working, and serious-minded President.

Hayes's father died before he was born, and he was raised by an uncle, who saw that young "Rud" got a good education. Hayes was a successful criminal lawyer in Cincinnati for several years, then fought in the Civil War, becoming a brevet major general in the Union Army.

Hayes was still at the front when he was elected to Congress. He later served two terms as governor of Ohio, and then the Republicans picked him to run for President.

The election was so close that everyone, even Hayes, thought he had lost to Tilden, the

Thomas Alva Edison developed the phonograph and invented the incandescent electric light bulb.

Democratic candidate. Hayes's backers challenged returns from three Southern states, and Congress established an Electoral Commission to investigate. It was finally decided, shortly before Inauguration Day, that Hayes, not Tilden, had been elected President.

In the White House, Hayes's wife, the former Lucy Webb, was known as "Lemonade Lucy" because she would not permit alcoholic beverages to be served. She would not allow card playing or dancing, and wore high-necked gowns for evening wear. Even so, social functions at the White House were popular and well attended. The Hayeses were friendly and hospitable and often the reception rooms served as "bedrooms" for overnight guests.

Hayes pledged protection of Negroes' rights, but he removed the last federal troops from the South to encourage self-government. From then until recently, the Southern states have voted as the "Solid South." Hayes insisted that appointments to government jobs should go to the best-qualified people.

During Hayes's term, one of the first telephones was installed in the White House. The inventor, Alexander Graham Bell, gave the President a personal demonstration. Thomas

Edison was also a White House guest. He showed Hayes his invention, the phonograph.

Hayes refused to run for a second term. He lived quietly in retirement at his home in Fremont, Ohio, until his death in 1893.

Rutherford Birchard Hayes
Important Events

- **Thomas A. Edison obtained patent for the phonograph (1878)**
- **Edison invented the first electric incandescent lamp (1879)**
- **New York City cited as the first U.S. city with a population of over one million (1880)**

James Abram Garfield

20th President

Born: November 19, 1831

Birthplace: Orange, Ohio

Previous experience: Teacher, military leader, Congressman, Senator

Political party: Republican

Term of office: March 4, 1881 – September 19, 1881

Died: September 19, 1881

James A. Garfield was the last President to be born in a log cabin.

James lost his father when he was only two years old. He worked hard as a boy, cutting wood, planting and reaping, and going to school whenever time allowed. When he was 16, he worked as a "tow boy," driving the horses and mules that pulled the boats on the Ohio Canal.

Garfield managed to graduate from college, working part of his way as a janitor, and became a professor of classics (Greek and Latin). Since he could write with either hand, he liked to amuse people by writing Greek with one hand and Latin with the other — at the same time!

When President Lincoln called for volunteers in 1861, Garfield joined up and showed unusual bravery. Even though his horse was shot from under him, Garfield delivered a message that saved his regiment from disaster. For that, he won a battlefield promotion to major general.

Garfield served as a member of Congress for 18 years. He became a recognized leader of his party and was made a U.S. Senator in 1880.

That was a presidential election year, and the Republicans could not decide on a candidate. They voted 35 times without coming to a decision. On the next ballot, they nominated Garfield, who won the election.

At this time in the 1880's, Civil Service jobs were not granted by taking merit exams. Instead, government jobs were often handed out to friends or political cronies by those in power. After Garfield's inauguration, office-seekers swarmed into the White House. People even stopped the President's carriage on the street to ask him for jobs.

The President could not give a job to everyone who asked. Among those he had to disappoint was a man named Charles Guiteau.

Less than four months after he had taken office, Garfield was waiting for a train at the station in Washington. Guiteau stepped forward and fired two shots, and Garfield slumped to the floor.

The wounded President was carried to the White House. Doctors were unable to locate and remove the bullets. (X-ray would not be invented for another 14 years.) Just 80 days after he was shot, Garfield died.

James Abram Garfield Important Event

- **American Red Cross organized (1881)**

Clara Barton was a Civil War nurse. Later, she founded the American Red Cross.

Chester Alan Arthur

21st President

Born: October 5, 1830
Birthplace: Fairfield, Vermont
Previous experience: Public official, Vice-President
Political party: Republican
Term of office: September 20, 1881 – March 3, 1885
Died: November 18, 1886

Garfield's assassination made Vice-President Chester Alan Arthur the nation's leader. Many people were afraid that he would do whatever the politicians told him to do. But Arthur surprised his critics with his honesty and courage.

A tall, handsome man, Arthur had become wealthy as a lawyer in New York City, and lived very well. He had a French cook and often spent two hours having dinner. He dressed elegantly in the latest fashions.

After becoming President, Arthur said the White House was too gloomy for him. He refused to live in the Executive Mansion until it was fixed over to suit his tastes. To make way for the expensive new furniture he ordered, 24 wagonloads of old things had to be carted away.

Arthur's political cronies were jubilant when he became President. They expected him to hand out jobs to his friends, as many politicians did at this time.

The Brooklyn Bridge in 1883, the year it opened. The nation's third oldest suspension bridge, it spans 1,595 feet over the East River, linking Manhattan and Brooklyn, NY.

But Arthur showed he had a mind of his own. He worked to bring about a fair system of filling government jobs and persuaded Congress to pass the nation's first "bi-partisan" Civil Service law. By this law, job-seekers had to pass tests to get certain types of government jobs, and they could not be removed from their jobs for political reasons.

Arthur also worked to modernize the Navy. He got new ships built to replace those that dated back to the Civil War.

Arthur would have liked to have run for the presidency in 1884. But although his good record pleased the people of the country, he had not pleased the leaders of the Republican Party. He was not considered as a candidate in 1884. Arthur's courage cost him his career in politics. He returned to his wealthy law practice in New York City for two more years.

Chester Alan Arthur
Important Events

- Civil Service Commission organized (1883)
- Territorial government in Alaska established (1884)
- Washington monument dedicated (1885)

Grover Cleveland

22nd and 24th President

Born: March 18, 1837
Birthplace: Caldwell, New Jersey
Previous experience: Lawyer, sheriff, mayor, governor
Political party: Democratic
Terms of office: March 4, 1885 – March 3, 1889 (first term)
March 4, 1893 – March 3, 1897 (second term)
Died: June 24, 1908

Grover Cleveland served one term as President, and then later served a second term. He was the only President ever to do this.

Cleveland was born in New Jersey, a preacher's son and one of nine children. He grew up in upstate New York and became a lawyer. As sheriff of New York's Erie County, Cleveland exposed many dishonest people. Later, he ran on his reform record and was elected mayor of Buffalo and then governor of New York State. He truly believed: "A public office is a public trust."

Cleveland's simple honesty and willingness to say "no" to politicians earned him many enemies, but more friends. He swept to victory in

1884, the first Democratic President in 25 years.

Cleveland was one of the hardest-working Presidents; he often stayed up until two o'clock in the morning, working on the nation's problems. He stood for old-fashioned honesty. He refused to grant Civil War pensions that seemed fraudulent, and he forced the railroad companies to give back 81 million acres of Western land.

Cleveland was also one of the largest Presidents, weighing in at around 260 pounds. Young

Settlers in Nebraska, 1886—a world away from the life in eastern cities.

relatives called him "Uncle Jumbo."

One of the most popular events of Cleveland's presidency was his White House marriage to 22-year-old Frances Folsom, the daughter of his former law partner. She softened the stern President's public image, but not enough to get Cleveland reelected in 1888. He lost to the Republican candidate, Benjamin Harrison.

Before leaving the White House, Mrs. Cleveland told her staff: "Take care of the furniture. . . We'll be coming back in four years." They did!

Cleveland's second four years as President were not as happy. A serious business depression set off the Panic of 1897. Banks and businesses failed by the hundreds, and millions of people were out of work. Cleveland maintained the gold reserve, but he never really solved the people's problems, like unemployment and small business failures.

Cleveland retired to his home in Princeton, New Jersey. He died in 1908. His last reported words were: "I have tried so hard to do right."

Grover Cleveland
Important Events

- **Chicago World's Fair opened (1893)**
- **Utah admitted as 45th state (1896)**

Benjamin Harrison

23rd President

Born: August 20, 1833
Birthplace: North Bend, Ohio
Previous experience: Lawyer, military leader, Senator
Political party: Republican
Term of office: March 4, 1889 – March 3, 1893
Died: March 13, 1901

Benjamin Harrison was "born into politics." His father was a Congressman from Ohio. His grandfather, "Old Tippecanoe," was William Henry Harrison, the ninth President of the U.S. And his great-grandfather signed the Declaration of Independence.

Ben went to school in a log schoolhouse, then studied law and became a lawyer in Indianapolis, where he campaigned for the Republican Party. He fought in the Civil War and then returned to his law practice.

As a public figure, Harrison was respected but not really liked. He seemed cold and unfriendly. Sometimes he kept visitors standing while he tapped his pencil, hoping they would take the hint and leave.

His reputation as an "iceberg" cost Harrison the election for the Indiana governorship in 1876, but he later made a successful bid for the U.S. Senate. This victory was his steppingstone to the presidency.

As President, Harrison took pride in his foreign policy. He established the basis of the Pan American Union and tried to get Hawaii annexed. Otherwise, he preferred to go along with Congress in handling problems of the day.

An early model of the Stanley steamer, a car that ran on steam; the two bearded men are the Stanley twins, who invented the car (1897).

During Harrison's administration, six new states were admitted to the Union: North Dakota, South Dakota, Montana, Washington, Idaho, and Wyoming. At last, the Bureau of the Census could report that the country was settled from coast to coast.

There were technological advances, too. Harrison was the first President to sign papers by electric light. He also happened to be the last President to wear a beard.

When Harrison ran for reelection in 1892, he was defeated by Grover Cleveland, the man he had narrowly beaten for the presidency four years earlier.

Benjamin Harrison
Important Events

- North Dakota, South Dakota, Montana, and Washington admitted to the Union as the 39th, 40th, 41st, and 42nd states (1889)
- Representatives of North and South American countries met in Washington for the first Pan American Conference (1889)
- Sherman Anti-trust Act enacted (1890)
- Idaho and Wyoming admitted to the Union as the 43rd and 44th states (1890)

William McKinley

25th President

Born: January 29, 1843
Birthplace: Niles, Ohio
Previous experience: Soldier, lawyer, Congressman, governor
Political party: Republican
Term of office: March 4, 1897 – September 14, 1901
Died: September 14, 1901

William McKinley was a kind, gentle man, as thoughtful of the men in his regiment during the Civil War as he was, later, of his invalid wife. One of our best-loved Presidents, he was an unlikely target for an assassin's bullet.

McKinley had been a lawyer, a Civil War soldier, a leader in Congress, and the governor of his state for two terms before being nominated for President.

As a presidential candidate in 1896, McKinley faced the fiery, young William Jennings Bryan. Bryan traveled across the country making speeches. But McKinley did not want to leave his wife; he campaigned near his home. Promising prosperous times and a "full dinner pail," McKinley won the election easily.

During McKinley's first term in office, the Spanish-American War began, with the slogan "Remember the Maine," after the U.S. battleship *Maine* was blown up in Havana harbor. The war lasted four months. Out of the peace settlement, the U.S. got Guam, Puerto Rico, and the Philippines.

McKinley defeated Bryan again in the election of 1900. But his second term ended tragically. The President was greeting people at the Pan-American Exposition of 1901 in Buffalo, New York, when a young man named Leon Czolgosz approached him. Czolgosz's right hand was wrapped in a handkerchief to conceal a gun. He fired two bullets into the President. Eight days later McKinley died.

William McKinley
Important Events

- Battleship *Maine* blown up in Havana harbor; and U.S. declared war on Spain (1898)
- Hawaii acquired by the U.S. (1898)
- Treaty of Paris, ending Spanish-American War, signed (1898)
- Guam, Puerto Rico, the Philippines, and American Samoa acquired by the U.S. (1899)

Theodore Roosevelt

26th President

Born: October 27, 1858

Birthplace: New York, New York

Previous experience: Rancher, governor,
  Assistant Secretary of the Navy, Vice-President

Political party: Republican

Term of office: September 14, 1901 – March 3, 1909

Died: January 6, 1919

As a child Theodore Roosevelt was too sickly to go to school. He had asthma, was near-sighted, and thin, weak, and nervous. Who could have guessed he would grow up to be our most vigorous President?

Luckily for "Teddy," his father was wealthy enough to build a gym on the second floor of their New York City home. There, young Ted pounded away at a punching bag, did chin-ups on an iron bar, and twirled Indian clubs.

In college Teddy took up boxing. Then he set out for the Dakota Territory to hunt buffalo and work on a cattle ranch as a cowboy.

Back in New York, Roosevelt served as a crime-busting police commissioner. He fired crooked cops and rounded up gangsters. "Teddy the Scorcher" became a New York hero.

President McKinley made Roosevelt Assistant Secretary of the Navy. Roosevelt called for a strong fleet. "Build a battleship in every creek!"

Immigrants from Europe look toward New York City's skyline. In the early 1900s, about 15,000 people arrived each day, seeking a new life in America.

he said. When the Spanish-American War broke out, Roosevelt organized the Rough Riders cavalry unit and led them in a famous charge up Cuba's San Juan Hill. Now a popular hero, he was elected governor of New York.

Crooked politicians called Roosevelt a "wild man." They put him up as Vice-President to get him out of the way. Then McKinley was shot, and suddenly, Theodore Roosevelt was President. At 42, he was the youngest one ever.

As President, Roosevelt pushed through the Panama Canal and opened a trans-Pacific cable. He declared himself an enemy of the giant trusts — big companies that controlled such industries as steel and coal. He fought their power and enforced anti-trust laws, believing the trusts might become more powerful than the government.

Roosevelt was one of the first Presidents to realize the importance of conserving our wilderness lands and natural resources. He added more than 125 million acres to the national forest system.

Roosevelt's six energetic children made news in the White House. The younger ones walked on stilts over the floors, slid down banisters, and took their pony upstairs in the elevator.

Roosevelt was elected to a full term in 1904. After he retired as President, he went to Africa on a long trip of hunting and exploration, and much later, explored the jungles of Brazil. But Roosevelt didn't like being on the political side-lines. In 1912 he ran for the presidency on the Progressive "Bull Moose" Party and lost. He died seven years later at his home in Oyster Bay, New York, one of our most colorful Presidents.

Theodore Roosevelt
Important Events

- First wireless signal received from Europe (1901)
- Departments of Commerce and Labor created (1903)
- Wright brothers' airplane flight at Kitty Hawk, North Carolina (1903)
- Panama Canal Zone acquired by the U.S. (1904)
- San Francisco earthquake (1906)
- Oklahoma admitted as 46th state (1907)
- American battleships departed on "round-the-world" cruise (1907)

William Howard Taft

27th President

Born: September 15, 1857

Birthplace: Cincinnati, Ohio

Previous experience: Lawyer, judge, governor of Philippines, Secretary of War

Political party: Republican

Term of office: March 4, 1909 – March 3, 1913

Died: March 8, 1930

"Taft is the most loveable personality I have ever known," said Theodore Roosevelt when he backed William Howard Taft for President.

Taft demonstrated personal qualities that Roosevelt greatly admired — a zest for life and good sportsmanship. Taft liked to laugh and have fun. He played a fast game of tennis and he was a graceful dancer in spite of his size. When the 1910 baseball season opened, he tossed out the first ball, a custom many Presidents have followed since then.

Taft was a huge man. He stood 6-foot-2 and weighed over 300 pounds. He ate steak for breakfast; when he was worried, he munched on salted almonds. At Yale University he played baseball and football. After graduation he became a lawyer and then a judge, like his father and grandfather before him.

In 1898, when the United States acquired the Philippines, President McKinley chose Taft to govern the islands. Taft made a good governor. He set up public schools and a court system in the Philippines, and helped establish hospitals and banks there.

After McKinley's assassination in 1901, President Theodore Roosevelt called Taft back to Washington to serve in his Cabinet. Roosevelt then helped Taft win the presidential election of 1908.

Roosevelt admired Taft's personal qualities, but he felt that Taft granted too many favors to businesses. He quarreled with Taft over tariff issues and his record on conservation. In 1912 Taft ran for a second term, strongly opposed by Roosevelt and his Progressive Party. Both men lost to Woodrow Wilson, the Democratic candidate.

Leaving the White House did not make Taft

unhappy. He called it "the lonesomest place in the world."

In 1921 President Harding appointed Taft Chief Justice of the United States Supreme Court. It was an assignment Taft liked much better than being President. He started each day

Henry Ford introduced a moving assembly line for the Model T chassis in August, 1913, cutting assembly time from 14 hours to 93 minutes.

at 5:15 in the morning and carried out his duties with great delight and enthusiasm.

Taft served as Chief Justice for nine years. He is the only American to have held both the highest executive and highest judicial office.

William Howard Taft
Important Events

- Peary discovered the North Pole (1909)
- New Mexico admitted as the 47th state (1912)
- Arizona admitted as 48th state (1912)
- Parcel Post service begins (1913)
- Sixteenth Amendment to the Constitution ratified, establishing the income tax (1913)

Woodrow Wilson

28th President

Born: December 28, 1856

Birthplace: Staunton, Virginia

Previous experience: Teacher, university president, governor

Political party: Democratic

Term of office: March 4, 1913–March 3, 1921

Died: February 3, 1924

B efore Woodrow Wilson was thrust into politics, he had spent over 30 years as a college student, professor, and university president.

The son of a minister and the grandson of a printer from Ireland, Wilson studied law, practiced it briefly, and then became a professor of law and political economy at Princeton University.

Wilson was strict with his students, yet he was named the most popular teacher there. In 1902 he was made president of the University.

Eight years later, when New Jersey's Democratic leaders were looking for a quiet, respectable candidate for governor of the state, they picked Wilson. Since he was inexperienced in real politics, they figured that he would do what he was told.

But Wilson surprised the politicians. He cleaned up the state and got rid of crooks in business and politics. He was so successful that the National Democratic Party, seeking a reform candidate to stand up to strong opposition, nominated Wilson for President. In 1912 Wilson defeated the Republican candidate Taft, and also Theodore Roosevelt, who ran on the Progressive Party ticket.

Suffragettes on parade. Women in 1912 marched for the right to vote. It became law in 1920.

As President, Wilson called for cuts in taxes on imported goods, stronger anti-trust laws, and our present Federal Reserve money system. In 1914 World War I broke out in Europe. Wilson was reelected in 1916 with the slogan, "He kept us out of war."

But early in his new term, German submarines sank several U.S. ships. Wilson sent warnings and then declared war on Germany on April 6, 1917. It was to be "a war to end war."

Early in 1918 Wilson proposed peace; in November the armistice was signed, and Wilson went to Paris for the peace talks. He called for a "League of Nations." The "League" would be a meeting place where nations could settle their quarrels without going to war.

Wilson was awarded the Nobel Peace Prize, but back home the U.S. Senate turned down Wilson's League of Nations plan. Bitterly disappointed, he traveled about the country pleading for his plan; then he suffered a stroke and never fully recovered. He died three years after leaving the White House.

"Ideas live; men die," Wilson once said. Today his idea for the League of Nations lives on as the United Nations.

Woodrow Wilson
Important Events

- Federal Reserve Act passed (1913)
- New York to San Francisco telephone demonstrated (1915)
- Liner *Lusitania* sunk by German submarine (1915)
- Senate ratified treaty to purchase Danish West Indies (Virgin Islands) (1916)
- U.S. declared war on Germany (1917)
- Armistice signed, ending World War I (1918)
- First meeting of League of Nations called (1920)
- Nineteenth Amendment to the Constitution ratified, giving women the right to vote (1920)
- First continental airmail flight from San Francisco to New York (1921)

Warren Gamaliel Harding

29th President

Born: November 2, 1865
Birthplace: Corsica, Ohio
Previous experience: Editor, lieutenant governor, Senator
Political party: Republican
Term of office: March 4, 1921 – August 2, 1923
Died: August 2, 1923

"I don't expect to be the best President, but I hope to be the best loved one," said Warren G. Harding. But even in that, he was doomed to disappointment.

Harding was born in 1865, seven months after the Civil War's end. At the age of 19, Harding and two friends borrowed $300 and bought a newspaper — the Marion (Ohio) *Star*. The paper became a big success, and through it Harding got to know Ohio's political leaders. They helped him become lieutenant governor of Ohio and, later, a U.S. Senator.

Tall, handsome, and friendly, Harding was a

very popular Senator. He had a smile and a pleasant word for everyone. The Republicans picked him to run for President in 1920.

In his campaign Harding promised a "return to normalcy." Americans, weary of wartime restrictions, swept Harding into office.

All went well at first. Wartime controls were taken off, taxes slashed. But President Harding surrounded himself with friends he trusted — and shouldn't have. Big oil scandals broke. One Cabinet member went to jail for taking bribes. Other officials were accused of stealing government funds.

Alarmed and feeling wronged, Harding set out on a speech-making tour to present his side of the story to America. During the trip, Harding suffered a heart attack and died suddenly, without having cleared his name.

Warren Gamaliel Harding
Important Events

- U.S., Japan, Italy, Great Britain, and France sign limitation agreement on naval armaments (1922)
- First woman Senator, Rebecca L. Felton of Georgia, appointed (1922)
- First woman member of Congress, Ella Mae Nola of California, took office (1923)

Calvin Coolidge

30th President

Born: July 4, 1872
Birthplace: Plymouth, Vermont
Previous experience: Lawyer, public official, governor, Vice-President
Political party: Republican
Term of office: August 3, 1923 – March 3, 1929
Died: January 5, 1933

If ever a man could cool down talk of bribes and scandal, it was Coolidge, the most thrifty of the Presidents.

Calvin Coolidge never wasted even words. "You must talk with me, Mr. Coolidge," a woman once pleaded. "I made a bet that I could get more than two words out of you." President Coolidge looked straight at her. "You lose," he said.

Coolidge was the only President to be born on the Fourth of July (in 1872). As a boy, he worked on the family farm in Vermont — taking the cows to pasture, planting crops, and doing various farm chores. After college he became a lawyer in Northampton, Massachusetts, where he met and married Grace Goodhue, who was a teacher of the deaf. He entered politics, and during the next 20 years, "Silent Cal," as he was called, served in 19 different public offices.

During his term as governor of Massachusetts, the police officers of Boston went on strike. Coolidge called out the state guard to keep order, saying, "There is no right to strike against the public safety by anybody, anywhere, anytime." This strong stand made Coolidge well known all over the country. The next year, he was elected Vice-President.

Coolidge was at his father's farm in Vermont when he was notified that President Harding had died. He got up in the middle of the night, dressed in his best black suit, and took the Oath of Office on the family Bible, in the presence of his notary public father and a few witnesses. Then the new President of the United States went back to bed.

As President, Coolidge obeyed the prohibition law. He did not serve alcoholic drinks. It is said that White House guests were sometimes served plain ice water — in paper cups! Still, with charming Grace Coolidge as first lady, social functions at the White House were popular and well attended.

Coolidge cleaned up the scandals and extravagances of the Harding administration and reduced the national debt.

A contented nation reelected Coolidge to a full term in 1924. But it was not a happy term for him. Early in the campaign, the Coolidges' 16-year-old son died of blood poisoning. "When he went," said Coolidge, "the power and the glory of the presidency went with him."

A proud, young Charles A. Lindbergh stands beside "The Spirit of St. Louis." In this frail plane he made the first transatlantic solo flight from the U.S. to Paris, France (1927).

In 1927 the Republicans wanted Coolidge to be their candidate once more. He answered, "I do not choose to run for President in 1928." When he left the White House, Coolidge was more popular than ever. Everyone had survived the jazz age of the 20's by "keeping cool with Coolidge."

Calvin Coolidge
Important Events

- Teapot Dome oil scandal revealed (1923 – 1924)
- Regular transcontinental air mail service established (1924)
- Liquid-fueled rocket flown (1926)
- Richard E. Byrd and Floyd Bennett made first flight over North Pole (1926)
- Charles Lindbergh completed first transatlantic solo flight (1927)

Herbert Clark Hoover

31st President

Born: August 10, 1874

Birthplace: West Branch, Iowa

Previous experience: Engineer, overseas U.S. Food and Relief administrator, Secretary of Commerce

Political party: Republican

Term of office: March 4, 1929 – March 3, 1933

Died: October 20, 1964

Herbert Hoover's personal story is one of rags to riches. He was an orphan who became a successful engineer and a millionaire by the age of 40. But the nation's story during his administration is one of riches to rags. Hoover faced a national depression that brought the United States almost to its knees.

The years of the Great Depression were the unluckiest of Hoover's long lifetime — which included four separate careers.

The son of an Iowa blacksmith, Hoover was born poor and was an orphan by the age of eight.

Raised by an aunt and uncle in Oregon, he studied to become a geologist and mining engineer at Stanford University. There he met and married Lou Henry, a fellow geologist, who traveled with him. Hoover's mining surveys took him all over the world. He discovered rich gold and iron deposits in Australia and China and became China's chief mining engineer.

Hoover's second career began after World War I, when he supervised the distribution of food to many millions of starving war refugees in Belgium and France. He extended the aid to Soviet Russia, telling critics: Starving people shall be fed, whatever their politics. Hoover served without pay and gave some of his own fortune to the cause.

He was Secretary of Commerce under Harding and Coolidge, but it was his fame as an organizer and administrator that led to Hoover's third career — as President. He was elected in 1928 by an electoral vote of 444 to 87.

Then came the economic crash of 1929. Very soon, more than 12 million Americans were out of work and banks and businesses were failing by the thousands. People expected a bold and decisive leader, but Hoover was cautious and traditional. He presented a program of public works and business financing to Congress, but he felt that aid — food and unemployment pay — should be at a local level. Congress and the nation waited for 1932, to elect a new President — Franklin Roosevelt.

The Empire State building in New York City opened May 1, 1931; 1,250 feet high with 102 stories, it was, for many years, the highest building around.

Hoover later found a fourth career under President Truman. He supervised a huge European relief program to feed starving victims of World War II. He was also coordinator of a committee to reorganize the executive branch of government. Hoover was in his 90th year when he died in New York City in 1964.

Herbert Clark Hoover
Important Events

- Stock market selling panic preceded the Great Depression (1929)
- Richard Byrd made South Pole flight (1929)
- Amelia Earhart completed first transatlantic solo flight by a woman (1932)
- Congress proposed 20th Amendment to the Constitution: President's term of office to begin on January 20 (rather than March 4) (1932); ratification completed January 23 (1933)

Franklin Delano Roosevelt

32nd President

Born: January 30, 1882
Birthplace: Hyde Park, New York
Previous experience: Public official, lawyer, governor
Political party: Democratic
Term of office: March 4, 1933 – April 12, 1945
Died: April 12, 1945

Much was expected of Franklin Roosevelt when he entered the White House. "Happy days are here again" had been the Democrats' campaign song. But this was the worst depression in the nation's history. No community was without its failed businesses, closed banks, and bread lines of the unemployed. Gray despair cloaked the entire nation.

Roosevelt talked to the people by radio in "fireside chats." (There was no television then.) His words were soothing and confident. "This great nation will revive," he declared. "The only thing we have to fear is fear itself."

Americans everywhere took hope. They would fight the Depression; they would defeat it.

Roosevelt matched his words with action. He launched a bold reform program called the "New Deal." He said it was meant to help all America, but especially the "forgotten man" — anyone who was poor and discouraged.

He set up huge public works programs to encourage business and consumer spending. He used public funds to create jobs for the unemployed, and provide food for the hungry, and shelter for the homeless. Farms and banks were saved.

"I am an old campaigner, and I love a good fight," Roosevelt once said. He tackled the Great Depression with a warrior's spirit. Later, he displayed that same spirit as he led the nation to victory in World War II against Hitler's Germany and Tojo's Japan.

Roosevelt's courage and zest for combat may have come from his long struggle against a crippling disease. In 1921 he suffered an attack of poliomyelitis, which cost him the use of his legs. But he never gave in to the disease, learning to get about by using heavy leg braces, crutches, and a wheelchair. He also learned to delegate work. His wife, Eleanor, traveled and represented him in many groups and appearances, and kept him in touch. He drew on the knowledge of many bright, young economists and political figures.

Roosevelt was elected to a second term in

Mrs. Roosevelt visiting Dust Bowl refugees. She traveled tirelessly, meeting and talking with people. During the war, she visited military hospitals and camps.

1936, a third term in 1940, and a fourth term in 1944. No other President served as long, and no other will. (See item 10, page 129.)

His fourth term was in its first months when Roosevelt attended a summit meeting at Yalta with Prime Minister Winston Churchill of Great Britain, and the Russian leader, Joseph Stalin. Roosevelt returned from the conference weary and ill. He died at Warm Springs, Georgia, less than a month before the war ended in Europe.

Jesse Owens won three gold medals (100-meter and 200-meter races and the long jump) in the 1936 Olympics in Germany under Hitler.

Franklin Delano Roosevelt
Important Events

- "Hundred Days" congressional session in which New Deal recovery measures enacted (1933)
- Tennessee Valley Authority (TVA), Civilian Conservation Corps (CCC), National Recovery Administration (NRA), and Public Works Administration (PWA) created (1933)
- Wiley Post made solo world flight (1933)
- Works Progress Administration (WPA) established (1935)
- Social Security Act passed (1935)
- National minimum wage enacted (1938)
- Opening of New York World's Fair (1939)
- Germany invaded Poland; Britain and France declared war on Germany; World War II began (1939)
- Registration for Selective Service began (1940)
- Japan attacked Pearl Harbor, Hawaii, Guam, and the Philippines; U.S. declared war against Japan; Germany and Italy declared war against the U.S. (1941)
- First demonstration of self-sustained nuclear chain reaction, Chicago (1942)
- Pay-as-you-go income tax bill signed (1943)
- Allied invasion of Europe in Normandy, France (1944)
- Churchill, Stalin, and Roosevelt confer at Yalta (1945)

Harry S. Truman

33rd President

Born: May 8, 1884

Birthplace: Lamar, Missouri

Previous experience: Farmer, store owner, judge, Senator, Vice-President

Political party: Democratic

Term of office: April 12, 1945 – January 20, 1953

Died: December 26, 1972

"I've got the most awful responsibility a man ever had. If you fellows ever pray, pray for me," Harry Truman told newspaper reporters when he became President. (Franklin Roosevelt had died in office on April 12, 1945.)

Although Germany surrendered on May 7, the U.S. was still fighting in the Pacific and Truman had to decide whether the new atomic bomb should be used against Japan. It would probably end the war and thus save lives. But no one knew exactly what its effects would be.

Finally, Truman gave the order. An atomic bomb was dropped on the city of Hiroshima. Three days later, another one was dropped over

Nagasaki. Japan surrendered six days after that, ending World War II, on August 15, 1945.

Harry S. Truman was born on a farm and managed it for his father for a time. He couldn't go to West Point because of poor eyesight, so he joined the National Guard, instead, and went overseas in World War I.

After the war, Major Truman ran a men's clothing store for a while. Then he went into

The first atomic explosion took place in the New Mexico desert on July 16, 1945. A mushroom cloud rose 41,000 feet into the air and left a half-mile wide crater with a glassy, radioactive crust.

politics in Missouri. He was elected to the U.S. Senate in 1936, and his fine record there led to his nomination as Vice-President with Franklin Roosevelt in 1944.

The next year, when Truman became President, he faced heavy postwar problems. Much of Europe lay in ruin. Millions were homeless and starving. Under the Truman Doctrine and, later, the Marshall Plan, America poured massive aid into the war-torn countries.

In 1948 the experts said that Truman had no chance of being reelected. But his blunt, no-nonsense manner appealed to the voters. "The buck stops here" was his slogan. Truman startled the experts and won the election.

To halt the spread of Communism, Truman supported foreign aid programs and entered into military alliances with Western European nations. When Communist North Korea invaded South Korea in 1950, the United Nations appealed for troops, and Truman sent a U.S. force to Korea.

Truman was often described as a "man of the people." He was a plain-spoken, small-sized man with a temper, but this "average man" became a strong, decisive President at a critical time in world history.

Harry S. Truman
Important Events

- Germany surrendered, ending World War II in Europe (1945)

- United Nations charter signed at San Francisco (1945)

- First atomic bomb detonated at Alamogordo, New Mexico (1945)

- U.S. dropped atomic bombs on Hiroshima and Nagasaki, forcing Japan to surrender (1945)

- Congress approved "Truman Doctrine," authorizing aid to Greece and Turkey (1947)

- Soviet Russia began Berlin blockade; U.S. and Great Britain began airlifting food to West Berlin (1948) (Ended 1949)

- Congress authorized Marshall Plan (1948)

- North Atlantic Treaty (NATO) signed by twelve nations (1949)

- First transcontinental television broadcast (1951)

- The 22nd Amendment ratified (1951). It stated that "no person shall be elected to the office of the President more than twice."

- Puerto Rico became a U.S. commonwealth (1952)

- U.N. appealed for peace troops; first U.S. ground troops sent to Korea (1950); peace talks began (1951); fighting ended (1953)

Dwight David Eisenhower

34th President

Born: October 14, 1890

Birthplace: Denison, Texas

Previous experience: Military leader, college president

Political party: Republican

Term of office: January 20, 1953 – January 20, 1961

Died: March 28, 1969

Dwight David Eisenhower was called "Ike" by his boyhood pals. It was a nickname that stuck. During his campaign for the presidency, crowds chanted, "We like Ike!" Even as President, people still spoke of him as Ike. They weren't being disrespectful. It was just the comfortable way they felt about this friendly man with the big grin.

Ike was two years old when his family moved from Texas to Abilene, Kansas, where he and his five brothers were raised. At Abilene High School, he starred in baseball and football, and worked in a dairy to save money for college.

Ike went to West Point, and for a while it looked as though he might become one of Army's great football stars. But he broke his knee, and the injury ended his football career. Later, he became a good golfer.

World War I was raging in Europe at the time Eisenhower graduated from West Point, but he never got into battle. Instead, he served as an instructor at different military bases.

With the beginning of World War II, Eisenhower's career took off. By 1942 he was commanding general of all of our military forces in Europe. A year later, President Roosevelt named him to direct the Allied invasion of France, the invasion that freed Europe of Hitler's control.

With victory in Europe, Eisenhower was hailed as America's No. 1 hero. Both the Democrats and Republicans asked him to be a presidential candidate in 1948. Ike refused. But in 1952 he agreed to run — as a Republican. That year and again in 1956, he defeated the Democratic candidate, Adlai Stevenson.

Although Ike had been a military leader for most of his life, as President he worked hard for peace. He traveled many thousands of miles on good-will missions. In a swing through Asia, millions cheered him in New Delhi and Teheran.

Also in his role as a peacemaker, Ike settled the Korean War. To ease tensions with the Soviet Union, he held a "summit conference" with the Russian Premier, Nikita Khrushchev.

Ike left the White House in January 1961 at the age of 70. He retired to his farm at Gettysburg, Pennsylvania. He died in 1969 at a military hospital near Washington.

General "Ike" Eisenhower, Commander-in-Chief of the Allied Expeditionary Force, reviewing American troops somewhere in England, early in 1944.

Dwight David Eisenhower
Important Events

- Korean War ended with signing of armistice (1953)
- First nuclear submarine, *Nautilus*, launched (1954)
- Supreme Court declared racial segregation in schools unconstitutional (1954)
- Eisenhower Doctrine bill signed, authorizing use of U.S. forces to assist Middle East nations threatened by Communist aggression (1957)
- First underground nuclear explosion (1957)
- Federal troops sent to Little Rock, Arkansas, to enforce integration of black students (1957)
- First American satellite, *Explorer I*, launched (1958)
- National Aeronautics and Space Administration (NASA) established (1958)
- Alaska and Hawaii admitted as the 49th and 50th states (1959)

John Fitzgerald Kennedy

35th President

Born: May 29, 1917
Birthplace: Brookline, Massachusetts
Previous experience: Congressman, Senator, author
Political party: Democratic
Term of office: January 20, 1961 – November 22, 1963
Died: November 22, 1963

When he took office, John F. Kennedy was 43, the youngest man ever elected President. With his boyish smile and unruly shock of brown hair, he looked even younger.

Jack Kennedy was the second oldest in a family of nine children. The father, Joseph P. Kennedy, had once served as ambassador to Great Britain. He was a millionaire many times over, but he wanted his children to be tough and competitive. Debates and competitive sports were a part of growing up a Kennedy. Young Jack was sent to exclusive private schools and attended Harvard University.

Although he enjoyed many advantages, Kennedy's success did not come easily. His back, injured in a sea battle during World War II, never stopped hurting him. The same year Jack was injured, his brother Joe was killed while piloting a plane over Belgium.

After the war Jack went home and won election to Congress and later to the Senate. At a friend's dinner party, he met stunning Jacqueline Lee Bouvier. They were married in 1953, and later had three children.

Senator John F. Kennedy, still a boyish Presidential candidate, with daughter Caroline and Jacqueline, his wife.

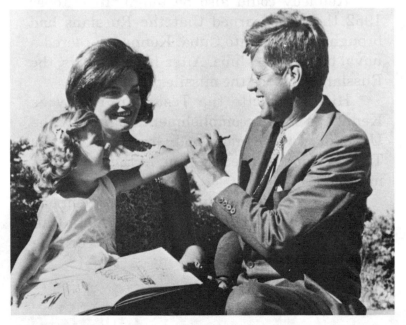

Kennedy was easily reelected to the Senate in 1958. Two years later, he was the Democratic presidential choice, opposing Richard Nixon. These two men were the first candidates to debate on television; the youthful, confident, witty Kennedy easily outshone the solemn, older Nixon.

Kennedy brought new style and vigor to the presidency. In his inaugural address, he declared, "Ask not what your country can do for you — ask what you can do for your country." He sponsored the Peace Corps and a space project to land a man on the moon. He and "Jackie" gave many concerts and encouraged the arts.

Kennedy could also be tough. In October 1962 the U.S. learned that the Russians had brought missiles into Cuba. Kennedy ordered a naval blockade of Cuba. After 13 tense days, the Russians removed the missiles.

Historians cite the Test Ban Treaty as Kennedy's chief accomplishment. Signed by the U.S., the Soviet Union, and Great Britain, the Treaty banned nuclear testing in the earth's atmosphere.

Six weeks after signing the Treaty, Kennedy went on a speech-making trip to Texas. In Dallas, on November 22, 1963, while he was driving in a motorcade, Kennedy was shot in the head by an assassin concealed in a nearby building. Kennedy died a few minutes later. The youngest man ever elected President, he was also, at 46, the youngest President to die in office.

John Fitzgerald Kennedy Important Events

- First live television press conference held (1961)
- Peace Corps created (1961)
- U.S. launched Bay of Pigs invasion, Cuba (1961)
- First U.S. astronaut, Commander Alan Shepard, rocketed into space (1961)
- East Germany closed border between East and West Berlin (1961)
- Lieut. Col. John Glenn, first U.S. astronaut to be put into orbit, orbited earth three times (1962)
- Supreme Court declared public school prayers to be unconstitutional (1962)
- More than 200,000 Americans participated in Civil Rights march, Washington, D.C. (1963)

Lyndon Baines Johnson

36th President

Born: August 27, 1908
Birthplace: Stonewall, Texas
Previous experience: Rancher, public official, Vice-President
Political party: Democratic
Term of office: November 22, 1963 – January 20, 1969
Died: January 22, 1973

As Vice-President and native Texan, Lyndon Baines Johnson — "L. B. J." — went with President John Kennedy on the fatal trip to Texas. On November 22, 1963, less than two hours after Kennedy had been shot, Johnson took the Oath of Office as President on board a plane that would rush him back to Washington.

A tall, rangy man, Johnson was 55 at the time, with more than thirty years' experience in politics — 12 as a U.S. Senator. He was a very hard worker, an arm twister, a man who could get things done. "Come now, let us reason together," he liked to say.

In his first months as President, Johnson displayed enormous skill in getting new laws passed. The Civil Rights Act of 1964, a major education bill, a new tax law, an anti-poverty program, and a food-stamp plan were all adopted.

When Johnson ran for reelection in 1964, he won an overwhelming victory. He pressed Congress to pass his "Great Society" program. Under its terms, every American could look forward to a good education, a comfortable and useful life, and an old age without worry.

Johnson might have earned high ranking among American Presidents were it not for one thing — the Vietnam War. He plunged the nation deeper and deeper into that tragic conflict. By the time he left office in 1969, close to a half million U.S. troops were in Vietnam, and angry war protestors were marching on Washington with bitter slogans and chants directed at L. B. J.

On March 31, 1968, Lyndon Johnson announced he would not run for reelection. He slipped away to the place he loved best — his ranch on the Perdenales River in Texas. He died there in 1973.

President Johnson shaking hands with Martin Luther King as he hands him a pen during the signing of the Civil Rights bill, July 2, 1964.

Lyndon Baines Johnson
Important Events

- Civil Rights Act signed into law (1964)
- Anti-poverty legislation signed by President (1964)
- "Great Society" program proposed by President in State of the Union message (1964)
- First American combat troops arrived in Vietnam (1965)
- *Early Bird*, world's first commercial satellite, launched (1965)
- President signed Medicare and voting rights bills (1965)
- Department of Housing and Urban Affairs created (1965)
- Artificial heart pump successfully implanted (1966)
- Dr. Martin Luther King assassinated (1968)
- Senator Robert F. Kennedy assassinated (1968)

Richard Milhous Nixon

37th President

Born: January 9, 1913

Birthplace: Yorba Linda, California

Previous experience: Lawyer, Congressman, Senator, Vice-President

Political party: Republican

Term of office: January 20, 1969 – August 9, 1974

Died: —

Richard M. Nixon, an acknowledged leader in foreign policy, was the first President ever to resign, and he resigned under a cloud.

He was born on a lemon farm in Yorba Linda, California, on the outskirts of Los Angeles. His ancestors were colonial settlers whose descendants kept moving west with the frontier. Nixon graduated from Whittier College, California, and then studied law in the East.

In both high school and college, Nixon was a champion debater. "He could take any side and win," said his debating coach.

After serving in the U.S. Navy during World War II, Nixon returned home to California and was elected to Congress in 1946. With national attention focused on his anti-Communist campaigns, he won a seat in the Senate and was Eisenhower's vice-presidential running mate in 1952.

Running for President in 1960, Nixon was the loser to John F. Kennedy in four televised debates and in the race for President.

Two years later, after losing in a race for governor of California, Nixon turned his back on politics. He joined a New York law firm. Little was heard from him for several years.

Then in 1968 Nixon staged a surprising comeback. He launched a smooth-running campaign for the presidency, and won in a close race against Vice-President Hubert Humphrey. (President Johnson did not enter the race.)

Nixon's first term as President was a triumph. He withdrew U.S. troops from Vietnam, winding down a war that had deeply divided the nation. In visits to China and the Soviet Union, he championed the cause of long-lasting peace. In 1972 Nixon was reelected by one of the greatest margins in U.S. history.

But trouble was brewing. Even before the

election, there was talk of a major scandal — Watergate. Police arrested five men who had burglarized the headquarters of the National Democratic Committee in the Watergate building in Washington and had installed wiretapping devices. As a Senate investigating committee probed for the truth, people close to Nixon, and Nixon himself, tried to cover up their involvement in this crime. Finally, in 1974 the House Judiciary Committee recommended adoption of impeachment proceedings.

U.S. Astronaut Neil A. Armstrong became the first man to set foot on the moon, July 20, 1969. Armstrong was commander of that famous Apollo 11 mission.

Some of Nixon's top assistants had by now been convicted of bribery, fraud, and the obstruction of justice and sent to prison.

Nixon himself resigned in disgrace on August 9, 1974. (He was later pardoned by President Ford.) In the years since then, Nixon has remained active, writing books and commenting on international relations.

Richard Milhous Nixon
Important Events

- Astronauts Neil Armstrong and Edwin Aldrin became the first to land on the moon (1969)
- U.S. began major withdrawals of troops from Vietnam (1970)
- President visited Russia and China; conferred with Chinese Premier Chou-En-Lai in Peking (1972)
- Justice Department announced FBI would investigate Watergate break-in (1972)
- Vietnam cease-fire agreement announced (1973)
- Vice-President Spiro T. Agnew resigned, to be replaced by Gerald R. Ford (1973)
- Supreme Court ruled that women must receive equal pay for equal work (1974)
- Seven former presidential aides indicted in Watergate conspiracy and President Nixon resigned (1974)

Gerald Rudolph Ford

38th President

Born: July 14, 1913
Birthplace: Omaha, Nebraska
Previous experience: Congressman, Vice-President
Political party: Republican
Term of office: August 9, 1974 – January 20, 1977
Died: —

When Gerald Ford advanced to the presidency, he was the first Vice-President not elected by the people to become President.

He was chosen by Richard Nixon to be Vice-President when Nixon's original Vice-President, Spiro Agnew, had to resign. The House of Representatives and the Senate approved Nixon's choice. Later, when Nixon himself left office, Ford moved into the White House.

A rugged looking, athletic man with a quick smile, Gerald Ford seemed to be just the person to restore the country's faith in the presidency.

He was open, honest, and decent.

Ford was a Midwesterner, born in Omaha, Nebraska, and raised in Grand Rapids, Michigan. During his high school and college years, Ford was a star football player. He graduated from the University of Michigan and Yale University Law School.

Ford's career as a lawyer was interrupted by World War II. Joining the Navy, he served for almost four years in the South Pacific. He was elected to Congress in 1948 and was then re-elected as a member of Congress 12 times.

Nixon picked Ford as his Vice-President in October 1973. After Nixon's resignation, the country turned to Ford with hope and relief.

A month after taking office, Ford granted Nixon a "full, complete, and absolute pardon" for the crimes he was said to have committed. For doing this, Ford was sharply criticized by many.

Ford's popularity also dwindled because of fuel shortages, inflation, and increasing unemployment. In foreign affairs, he followed Nixon's policy of holding talks with the Russian and Chinese heads of state.

In the Presidential election of 1976, Ford faced an uphill battle against Jimmy Carter, a Democrat from Georgia. They debated three

times on national television. Ford slowly gained
ground but still lost in a close election.

Gerald Rudolph Ford
Important Events

- President granted unconditional pardon to
  former President Nixon (1974)
- Nelson Rockefeller sworn in as Vice-
  President (1974)
- Construction of Alaskan oil pipeline
  started (1975)
- U.S. involvement in Vietnam ended with
  helicopter evacuation of last remaining
  Americans (1975)
- Bicentennial of United States of America,
  marking 200 years since Declaration of
  Independence was signed (1976)

James Earl Carter

39th President

Born: October 1, 1924

Birthplace: Plains, Georgia

Previous experience: Engineer, naval officer, farmer, businessman, state senator, governor

Political party: Democratic

Term of office: January 20, 1977 – January 20, 1981

Died: —

A dark horse candidate who often spoke of himself as a "simple country boy," Jimmy Carter was the first Southerner in more than a century to become President.

He grew up in the small town of Plains, Georgia (population 550), and took over the family's peanut business there when his father died. He was an active civic leader in his home town, a school-board member, and a deacon of the local church. He married Rosalynn Smith, also from Georgia, and they had four children.

But the "simple country boy" also graduated with honors from the U.S. Naval Academy. He served in the Navy's nuclear submarine program and studied nuclear physics. Returning home after resigning his naval commission, Carter became a state senator at 38, and governor of Georgia at 46.

He was serving as governor when he decided to run for President, even though he was practically unknown outside the South. Traveling almost alone and carrying his own luggage, Carter crisscrossed the nation, promising to restore to the presidency "all that is good and decent and honest and truthful and fair and competent. . . ."

President Carter, Egyptian President Anwar Sadat, and Israeli Prime Minister Menachem Begin shake hands after signing the Mideast peace treaty in March, 1979.

To Americans still reeling from the Watergate scandal, Carter's message had great appeal. At the Democratic convention in 1976, he was nominated on the first ballot and then won a narrow victory over Gerald Ford.

Carter took office with the well wishes of the nation. People liked it that he and his wife had walked and waved in the Inaugural Parade, that their nine-year-old daughter Amy attended a public school, and that Carter jogged for exercise.

Carter worked hard as President to combat inflation and unemployment, but he failed to solve these problems. In foreign policy, he played a key role in bringing about a peace treaty between Israel and Egypt, but this bright success was overshadowed by a grim setback toward the final year of his term. Iranian students seized the U.S. Embassy in Iran and held 52 Americans hostage. Americans were shocked and angry.

Negotiations for the release of the hostages dragged on for more than a year. Carter's popularity nose-dived. Freeing the hostages became an important campaign issue in 1980. Carter finally succeeded in obtaining their release on Inauguration Day, 1981, as the new President, Ronald Reagan, was taking office.

James Earl Carter
Important Events

- President established "human rights" as a key element in his foreign policy (1977)
- U.S. officially recognized the People's Republic of China (1979)
- Canal Zone ceded to Republic of Panama (1979)
- U.S. Embassy personnel taken hostage in Iran (1979)
- More than 125,000 refugees fled Cuba for the U.S. (1980)
- Iran returned hostages to the U.S. (1981)

Ronald Reagan

40th President

Born: February 6, 1911

Birthplace: Tampico, Illinois

Previous experience: Sports announcer, actor, union official, governor

Political party: Republican

Term of office: January 20, 1981 – January 20, 1989

Died: —

At 69, Ronald Reagan was the oldest man ever elected President. But he seemed much younger, thanks to his vigorous and athletic appearance.

Ronald Reagan was born in Tampico, Illinois, the son of a shoe clerk whose income barely supported the family. His mother loved the theater, and from her, Ronald, or "Dutch," as he was called, developed an interest in acting.

In high school, Dutch appeared in several school plays, besides playing football and being captain of the swimming team. Later, he had leading roles in many college plays.

After graduation Reagan became a radio

sports announcer. In 1937, when the Chicago Cubs went to spring training camp in California, Reagan went with the team to broadcast their games. While there, he made a screen test for a major motion picture studio. This led to an acting career; he appeared in more than 50 movies and hosted two dramatic shows on television.

Reagan was active with the Screen Actors Guild, a labor union of movie and television performers, serving for six years as president.

At the same time, Reagan was also active in

President Reagan and Chief Justice Warren Burger pose with the first woman Justice of the Supreme Court, Sandra Day O'Connor, in 1981.

national politics. He campaigned in 1948 for Harry Truman, a Democrat. But during the 1950's, as his views became more conservative, Reagan began supporting Republicans.

When someone suggested that he run for governor of California, Reagan laughed. He felt he didn't have a chance of winning. But when he tried in 1966, he defeated the Democratic candidate by a landslide. He was reelected governor in 1970 and served until 1975.

A year later, Reagan campaigned for the Republican presidential nomination. He lost to President Ford, who, in turn, lost the presidency to Jimmy Carter.

In 1980 Reagan tried for the Republican nomination again and won. President Carter, whose term had been dogged by issues he could not settle, was no match for Reagan. The former actor showed himself to be a skillful campaigner. He spoke firmly on issues, and, with his warm smile and easy, conversational style, he projected confidence. He won, hands down.

As President, Reagan defended basic values — work, the family, and patriotism. He slashed taxes, but also cut spending for welfare and unemployment programs. His economic policies were called "Reaganomics."

From the beginning, Reagan took a tough

stand toward the Soviet Union. Warning that the U.S. must keep militarily strong in order to have lasting peace, he called for stepped-up spending on missiles, bombers, and other weapons.

Out of a series of summit meetings with Soviet leader Mikhail Gorbachev came a nuclear missile treaty, which Reagan and Gorbachev signed in 1987. It called for the elimination of an entire class of nuclear-armed missiles.

As Reagan's administration drew to a close, he was given good marks on economic issues. But his success in reducing the likelihood of nuclear war was said to be his greatest success.

Ronald Reagan
Important Events

- World's first reusable aircraft, space shuttle *Columbia*, sent into space (1981)
- Sandra Day O'Connor became first woman justice of the U.S. Supreme Court (1981)
- First permanent artificial heart implanted (1982)
- Peacekeeping force of U.S. Marines assigned to Lebanon (1983) (Withdrawn, 1984)
- U.S. troops invaded Grenada and ousted Cuban forces (1983)
- President met with Soviet leader Mikhail Gorbachev in Washington, and signed a nuclear missile treaty (1987)

George Herbert Walker Bush

41st President

Born: June 12, 1924

Birthplace: Milton, Massachusetts

Previous experience: Vice-President; Congressman; ambassador; Chairman, Republican National Committee; Director, Central Intelligence Agency

Political party: Republican

Term of Office: January 20, 1989 –

Died: —

George Herbert Walker Bush, whose long record in politics and government included eight years as Ronald Reagan's Vice-President, was elected the 41st President in 1988. He became the first Vice President since Martin Van Buren to be elected directly to the presidency.

George Bush was born in Milton, Massachusetts. He grew up with his sister and three brothers in Greenwich, Connecticut, a wealthy suburb of New York City.

At Phillips Academy in Andover, Massachusetts, where he was known as "Poppy," Bush was captain of the basketball and soccer teams, played baseball, and served as president of the senior class.

When Bush graduated from Andover in 1942, World War II was raging. Instead of going to college, Bush enlisted in the Navy as a pilot. He was, for a time, the war's youngest Navy pilot.

After the war, Bush went to college at Yale. An honors student, he graduated in 1948 with a degree in economics. He turned down an offer to join his father in a banking career in favor of starting a new life with his wife and young son in the oil fields of west Texas.

Bush's father became a U.S. Senator from the state of Connecticut in 1962. Not long after, George became interested in a political career. He ran for the Senate in 1964, and lost. But the next time he ran for office, in 1966, he won a seat in the U.S. House of Representatives from the Seventh District of Texas. He served two terms.

After another unsuccessful try for the Senate, Bush was named by President Nixon to be U.S. Ambassador to the United Nations, a post he held for two years.

Bush served as Chairman of the Republican National Committee during the years the Watergate scandal was breaking. After a year as U.S. envoy to China, Bush was called home to head the Central Intelligence Agency, the CIA, during troubled times for the agency.

Bush made a run for the presidency in 1980, but the Republican nomination went to Ronald Reagan. Reagan then asked Bush to run with him as his vice-presidential candidate.

As Reagan's Vice-President, Bush was always loyal and hard-working, supporting the President's policies even when he may not have agreed with them. Reagan showed his gratitude when Bush ran for the presidency in 1988. He not only gave Bush his endorsement but campaigned for him from one coast to the other.

In Bush's first years in office, he benefited from a solid economy and the collapse of Communism in Eastern Europe. His popularity soared to even greater heights after he sent U.S. forces to the Persian Gulf in 1990 following Iraq's invasion of Kuwait. Allied forces quickly retook Kuwait early in 1991.

Bush was much less successful at home. He promised he would not ask for new taxes — and he did. The economy slumped. Social problems got worse. Criticized for his caution and lack of leadership, Bush faced an uphill struggle in his bid for reelection in 1992.

ELECTORAL VOTES FOR EACH STATE

State	Votes	State	Votes
Alabama	9	Nebraska	5
Alaska	3	Nevada	4
Arizona	8	New Hampshire	4
Arkansas	6	New Jersey	15
California	54	New Mexico	5
Colorado	8	New York	33
Connecticut	8	North Carolina	14
Delaware	3	North Dakota	3
District of Columbia	3	Ohio	21
Florida	25	Oklahoma	8
Georgia	13	Oregon	7
Hawaii	4	Pennsylvania	23
Idaho	4	Rhode Island	4
Illinois	22	South Carolina	8
Indiana	12	South Dakota	3
Iowa	7	Tennessee	11
Kansas	6	Texas	32
Kentucky	8	Utah	5
Louisiana	9	Vermont	3
Maine	4	Virginia	13
Maryland	10	Washington	11
Massachusetts	12	West Virginia	5
Michigan	18	Wisconsin	11
Minnesota	10	Wyoming	3
Mississippi	7		
Missouri	11		
Montana	3	TOTAL:	538